# Reference Modeling

Jörg Becker · Patrick Delfmann
(Editors)

# Reference Modeling

Efficient Information Systems Design
Through Reuse of Information Models

With 55 Figures and 5 Tables

Physica-Verlag

A Springer Company

Professor Dr. Jörg Becker
Dr. Patrick Delfmann
Westfälische Wilhelms-Universität Münster
European Research Center for Information Systems (ERCIS)
Leonardo-Campus 3
48149 Münster
Germany
becker@ercis.uni-muenster.de
delfmann@ercis.uni-muenster.de

Library of Congress Control Number: 2007930666

ISBN 978-3-7908-1965-6  Physica-Verlag Heidelberg New York

Physica-Verlag is a part of Springer Science+Business Media

springer.com

© Physica-Verlag Heidelberg 2007

Production: LE-TEX Jelonek, Schmidt & Vöckler GbR, Leipzig
Cover-design: WMX Design GmbH, Heidelberg

SPIN 12080366      134/3180YL - 5 4 3 2 1 0      Printed on acid-free paper

# Preface

The development of information models is a complex and time consuming task. Therefore reusability of information models has been discussed in science and practice for many years. Reference information models (shortly: reference models) are information models that are developed with the aim of being reused for different but similar application scenarios. The benefit that is promised by the use of reference models is primarily time and cost savings, since part of the reference models is reused. The topic of reference modeling is addressed in this book from different perspectives:

Besides *reference modeling languages* that provide special modeling language concepts for the development and application of reference models, *reference modeling methodologies* are discussed that provide in addition procedure models for the construction and application of reference models. Moreover, particular *reference models* are discussed and evaluated that are developed using a special language resp. methodology and that represent a set of different but similar application scenarios.

OLIVER THOMAS discusses concepts in order to derive and maintain reference model versions. He introduces reference modeling language extensions, an according reference model repository architecture and a *reference model version management* capable modeling tool. JÖRG BECKER, PATRICK DELFMANN and RALF KNACKSTEDT present a special reference modeling language that allows for generating reference model variants for different purposes easily. They combine different paradigms of model adaptation such as Configuration, Aggregation, Instantiation, Specialization and Conclusion by Analogy in an approach called *adaptive reference modeling*. A similar approach in order to build reference model variants is discussed by FLORIAN GOTTSCHALK, WIL M. P. VAN DER AALST and MONIQUE H. JANSEN-VULLERS. They propose a foundational approach towards *configurable Process Models*, which they illustrate with the example of Event-Driven Process Chains. TOBIAS RIEKE AND CHRISTIAN SEEL show how the life cycle of configurative reference models – requirements definition, construction, adaptation, implementation and application – can be supported by *controlling* concepts in order to be able to produce improved reference models.

A particular Reference Information Model for Enterprise-Wide Project Planning, Controlling and Coordination in Matrix Project Organizations (RefMod$^{PM}$) is introduced by FREDERIK AHLEMANN. He presents the framework of the model as well as detailed model examples. Finally, TILO BÖHMANN, MICHAEL SCHERMANN and HELMUT KRCMAR address the problem that the advantages that are associated with reference models are currently not reflected in documented usage of reference models in practice. Therefore, they claim that empirical evaluations of reference models are needed. They provide a framework for the evaluation of reference models and apply the framework for a reference model for Service Data Management (SDM).

The contributions of this book have been submitted to the 9th Conference on Reference Modeling (RefMod) 2006 and have been selected in a rigorous, double blind peer-review process. The RefMod 2006 has taken place as a track on the Multi-Conference on Information Systems (Multi-Konferenz Wirtschaftsinformatik, MKWI 2006) the 20th of February 2006. We would like to thank all authors, organizers and involved persons that have made this book possible. Finally, we thank the organizers of MKWI 2006. The conference has provided a competent and reliable environment for RefMod as already in the past years.

Münster, April 2007                                                    Jörg Becker
                                                                  Patrick Delfmann

# Contents

## Adaptive Reference Modeling: Integrating Configurative and Generic Adaptation Techniques for Information Models

Jörg Becker, Patrick Delfmann, Ralf Knackstedt ................................. **27**

## Configurable Process Models – A Foundational Approach

Florian Gottschalk, Wil M. P. van der Aalst,
Monique H. Jansen-Vullers ................................................. **59**

**Supporting Enterprise Systems Introduction
by Controlling-Enabled Configurative Reference Modeling**

## RefMod<sup>PM</sup>: Reference Information Model for Enterprise-Wide Project Planning, Controlling and Coordination in Matrix Project Organizations

## Application-Oriented Evaluation of the SDM Reference Model: Framework, Instantiation and Initial Findings

# Version Management for Reference Models: Design and Implementation

Oliver Thomas

*Abstract:* *The central idea in reference modeling is the reutilization of the business knowledge contained in a reference model for the construction of specific information models. The user's task in reference model-based construction is the adaptation of the reference model. The derivation of specific models from reference models characterized as such corresponds with the creation of reference model variants. Research on the design of such variant constructions generally assumes an unchangeable stock of reference models. The potentials available in the management of these variant constructions, which reflect the changes in reference models through time and, in doing so, their evolutionary development, has not yet been tapped into. The article at hand analyzes this problem and presents a concept for the version management of reference models as a solution. The task to be mastered using the proposed approach will be concretized using data structures and a system architecture, as well as prototypically implemented in the form of an application system.*

## 1    Initial Situation and Problem

It is generally accepted that models cannot be explicitly attributed to their originals – models fulfill their function in time; within certain time intervals [Stac73, pp. 132f.]. This assertion from STACHOWIAKs General Model Theory also applies to the focus of this article, the reference model-term. Reference models are reusable representations of abstract know-how for a given application domain [FeLo04; Schü98; Thom95b; Broc03]. The knowledge and experience in these models is not unchangeable, so that reference models themselves are subject to change throughout time. For models constructed within the framework of the two processes in reference modeling, development and usage, these changes generally occur in two manners. *First*, if, within the framework of an evaluation, one notices during the development of a reference model that the model being constructed does not fulfill the defined requirements, then one must return to preliminary phases. This generally results in revisional constructions, which replace the construction results evaluated. And *second*, revisional reference model constructions are also generated when using reference models to derive specific models. These revisional reference model constructions often differ only slightly from one another, depending on their use. Both of these aspects lead to a differentiation between version and variant constructions.

Available reference modeling literature focuses on variant management [BeDK02; BeDK04; BDKK02; Schü98; ThAH03; ThAS05; BrBu04]. The terminological difference between variants and versions is alluded to in literature [EsGK02, p. 96; Schl00, p. 74; Broc03, p. 260; WSHF98, p. 63], however the design of a version management for reference models has occurred in rudimentary form only. The task of the article at hand is to meet these concerns with the design and prototypical implementation of a version management tool for reference models.

## 2 Methodical Considerations and Course of the Analysis

The goal of this analysis is the design and realization of an information system for the support of a version management for reference models. Established procedure models are already in existence for the information system development required here. The task of these models is to secure the continuous description of the process, from the business requirements to the technical implementation.

This analysis will use the phase model for the architecture of integrated information systems (ARIS) from SCHEER [Sche02, pp. 38ff.].The ARIS-phase model differentiates between the description levels "requirements definition", "design specification" and "implementation". In the requirements definition-phase, the business concept to be supported is described in semi-formal languages. The design specification-phase adapts the requirements-description to basic interfaces in information technology. Finally, in the implementation-phase, the design specification is transferred to concrete information-technical components.

The requirements definition is especially important for achieving our goal because *first*, it can be seen as a long-term bearer of business concepts (sub-goal "design") and *second*, it acts as a starting point for further steps towards the technical implementation (sub-goal "realization").

This results in the following outline for the article at hand. Section 3 lays a foundation for the terms used here by first explaining the terms "information" resp. "reference model" and then differentiating between the terms "variant" and "version" in the context of reference modeling. Due to the methodical procedure selected for the design of the reference model version management, an information model will be constructed in Section 4, which represents the versioning for reference models on a conceptual level. In Section 5, this description will be adapted to general IT-interfaces class *Information Model*. The diagram-like management of versions using version graph-models – which requires not only recording the respective construction results, but also recording the relations existing between these (cf. also Figure 3) – can now be annotated by a predecessor-successor-re-lationship in the form of the recursive (0..*):(0..*)-association class *Version Structure* using the corresponding role on the class *Information Model-Version* (cf. Figure 4).

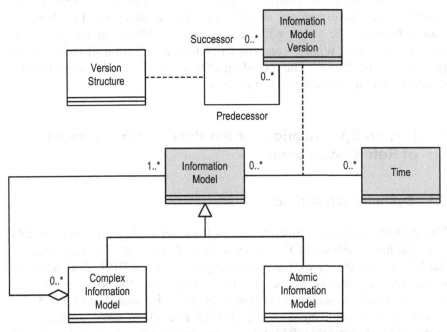

**Figure 4:** Extension of the management of model-versions through version graphs

The essential requirements on the conception of system functionality for the management of information model-versions as a sub-aspect of reference model development and usage are herewith defined. In addition to the construction results represented by models, information must be recorded about revisional constructions carried out on a model within the framework of a modeling project such as content, reason, time, those responsible, etc. The chronicle of these revisional constructions and the reasons for making them allows the retrospective analysis of the same and provides information for decision-making processes in future developments [EsGK02, p. 93].

This applies to not only reference model development and usage, but also to the implementation phase of a constructed to-be-model in an enterprise or the implementation of an application system, which both potentially follow these processes. If for example, within the framework of a reference process model adaptation, the required processes are selected resp. unnecessary processes removed using typological features of an enterprise and an automatic control system, then the connection between the requirements used and the process-structures selected is lost in the process. It is however, exactly this information, which is needed for further revisional constructions, as well as for the remodeling of a process already being carried out in an enterprise. Information about the reasons for the structure of a certain process, as well as for its modification – the "Why" – should therefore be saved with the model, in addition to the processes themselves – the "What" – and the rules for the selection of the required processes – the "How". The recording of this information is guaranteed by the data structure represented in Figure 4.

# 5   Design Specification for the Version Management of Reference Models

## 5.1   System Architecture

The primary technical aspect of the tool for versioning reference models refers to the definition of the technological platform, the identification of the IT-components, as well as the description of their DP-logical relationships. The architecture of the system referred to in the following as the *reference model management system* (RMMS) is illustrated in Figure 5.

The system architecture of the RMMS is a client/server-architecture. Due to the multitude of RMMS-system elements these are "classically" structured in three layers – the data management, application and presentation layers.

The data management-layer of the RMMS-system architecture is divided up into database and file management. While the structured data (human resource and customer data, as well as as-is and reference models) is managed in relational databases, the weakly structured data (text documents, spread sheets, presentation graphics, images, video and audio files, as well as links to further documents) is stored in a file system.

The data management-layer differentiates between four databases – an enterprise-wide human resource database, an enterprise-wide customer database, an as-is-model database and a reference model database. The reference model database in particular is a systematized collection of reference models (reference model library). It stores the reference model constructs, as well as their structural relationships, model attributes such as name, identification number, type of model (for example: EPC or ERM), description, time of creation, originator, last modification or last processor. The customer model database is also a model database, as is the case with the reference model database. It contains documented as-is-models, i. e. sections of the customer's enterprise-structure interpreted by the creator of the model at the time of modeling. It makes no difference whether the customer is internal or external.

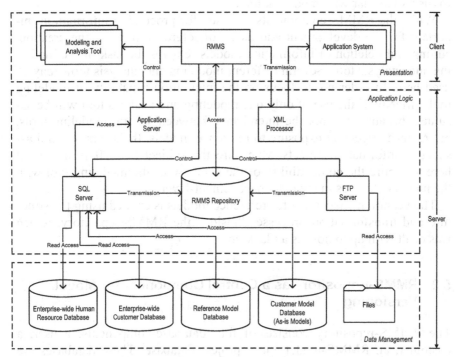

**Figure 5:** RMMS-system architecture

The external databases in Figure 5 are represented as a logical unit for purposes of simplicity, which however, as a rule, consist physically of several distributed databases. For example, the reference model database could consist of several external databases. This is the case when, in modeling projects, reference models from different modeling tools are used and each manage the models in their own databases.

The application layer comprises the server-services and data (RMMS-repository) used to carry out the technical tasks. The programs in this layer receive the user's (clients) instructions and carry them out on the relevant data. By using a client/server-architecture, several applications and users can access the same database at the same time and process it.

The components of the RMMS, with which the user has contact, are assigned to the presentation layer. They make the input and output more user-friendly and are represented by a graphic interface. The operational concept of the RMMS and its graphic user interface should be adapted to the interface design of established modeling and analysis tools. This way, for the user, the separate systems appear to be a logical entity – from the technological point of view. This also makes access to the RMMS easier for users familiar with modeling tools.

While the RMMS-components are used for processing information important for the development and usage of reference models, the creation, editing and deletion of information models remains the task of the modeling and analysis tool. Several different modeling and analysis tools may be used here. In order not to focus on the integration capability of modeling tools [MeNü03] the use of only one modeling and analysis tool will be assumed, because it is not the interchange between several modeling tools, but rather the general exposure to reference models, their versions and associated information objects which are the subject here. It is important here to secure the compatibility of the database of the modeling tool with the model databases in the data management-layer.

The version management for reference models is created using the structure and transformation processes "inside" the RMMS-repository, which was dealt with up to now as a black box.

## 5.2   RMMS-Repository as a Central Component for Model Versioning

The RMMS-repository consists of four database-components: a user, a customer, an RMMS-model and a project database. These databases are managed by the server plotted in Figure 5 and show relations to the external databases described above, as well as to the external file system. The data access and transfer of the server has already been discussed. For purposes of clarity, only the relations between the components of the repository and the components of the data management-layer have been accentuated graphically in Figure 6.

The system-users are created in the user database and are authenticated with it. The user database is a database derived from the enterprise-wide human resource database. Beyond the "business card" managed in the enterprise-wide human resource database, the user database of the RMMS contains the personal profile of the user (for example: start and standard settings of the RMMS-user interface, technical interests), as well as authorizations given to the user regarding the manipulation of data. Basic rights of disposal are the reading, creation, modification and deletion of objects.

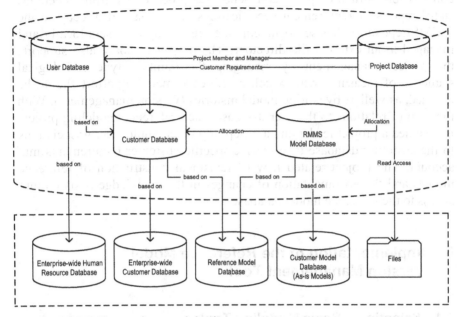

**Figure 6:** RMMS-repository and databases

The customer database is based on the external enterprise-wide customer database. The fact that customers appear as users of the RMMS is indicated by the relation between the customer database and the user database.

In addition to the "pure" model-data, the RMMS-model database also manages information about the construction of versions during the project. On the one hand, it adopts models from the external reference model database and on the other, the consideration of already existing information systems for reference model usage requires accessing the customer's external as-is-model database (reverse engineering).

The transfer of the model-data into a logical structure allows the simple connection to further external model databases in the system architecture. It also allows the RMMS-user to carry out the same functions on all models. This comprises not only the version management of the models, but also searching resp. navigating in the model databases.

Because the information models are not created and processed with the RMMS, but rather with the modeling tool, it appears expedient to allow the RMMS read-access to only the external databases.

The project database is at the center of the RMMS-repository in Figure 6. It manages internal and external reference modeling project-tasks between organizational units by storing data, such as the project name, type, goal, period, status or progress. Project documents, such as the project commission, structure plan, and schedule, proceedings from meetings, status reports or requirement specifications are not stored directly in the RMMS-repository. These documents are created by the users locally and managed in an external file directory. The project database also supports the project management by managing the number, type and logical sequence of measures with which a reference modeling-effort should be realized, as well as by storing model histories (version management). With the help of relations to the user database, each reference modeling project is assigned a project leader and a group of project employees. Associations to the customer database take service-specific customer requirements into account. The project-related new or revisional construction of reference models and the documentation of changes in the knowledge basis require access to the reference model database.

## 6    Implementation of the Reference Model Version Management Tool

### 6.1    Selecting a Basis Modeling Tool

The concept introduced for the version management of reference models was developed up to now independent of modeling languages, methods and tools. This applies to the construction of the conceptual models in Section 4, as well as to the design of the system architecture and the RMMS-repository in Section 5.

Because established products exist in the field of modeling [Sinu04], a complete new development of the RMMS is not necessary, but rather an extension of the existing systems. The functionalities necessary for the development and usage of reference models, which for example, make the revisional construction of models possible have already been implemented in the respective tools. Functionalities, which on the other hand serve the documentation of the construction process or a certain procedure in reference model usage must be re-implemented as necessary. The RMMS is therefore implemented as an integrated component of a professional tool for modeling business processes. The ARIS-Toolset from IDS Scheer, Inc. has been selected as a basis modeling tool. The ARIS-Toolset is a software system for the analysis, creation and navigation of business processes [IDS03]. It is based on the research of the Institute for Information Systems (IWi) in Saarbruecken. The following are factors, which were decisive for choosing the ARIS-Toolset as the basis modeling tool:

1. IDS Scheer, Inc. and the Institute for Information Systems (IWi) are both located in Saarbruecken. This naturally facilitates the intensive dialogue between employees and software developers on the topic of reference modeling, as well as the support of reference modeling with tools as seen by the user. In addition, travel costs were kept at a minimum due to the close proximity of these two institutions.
2. Since 1994, IDS Scheer, Inc. has provided several reference models created with the ARIS-Toolset [IDS05]. These were made available by the company and were used for testing purposes within the framework of the research project which builds the foundation of this article.

## 6.2  Graphic Representation of the Models

The work area of the RMMS is divided up into an explorer and a viewer (cf. Figure 7). All of the information models managed by the RMMS are displayed in the explorer. This applies to the reference models constructed in development projects, as well as enterprise-specific models created in application projects.

The index-card system of the RMMS serves the management of important information for the development and usage of reference models. The information models managed by the RMMS are characterized on the index card "Overview". The other index cards serve the graphic model representation ("Graphic"), the representation of model attributes ("Attributes") and the support of distributed construction processes ("Collaboration"). In Figure 7, the index card "Graphic" is activated. It gives users access to the versioning functionalities. The functionalities, which support the graphic representation of the models in the RMMS will therefore be discussed first as seen in the screenshot in Figure 7.

While the graphic representation of the information model is displayed in the left part of the index card, the attributes of the model components selected by the user are displayed on the right side. For navigation within the graphic, the user is given different functionalities. In the example in Figure 7, the Version 1.2 of a reference model framework for event management which, due to its form, is referred to as "Event-E", is selected. The project, which serves the development of a reference model for the application domain "event management" was carried out at the Institute for Information Systems. Here, we will abstract from the functional aspects of this reference model. The event management reference model is documented in [ThAS05].

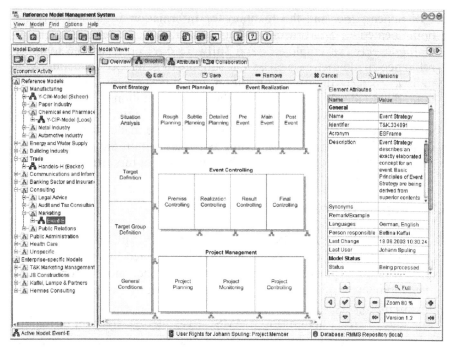

**Figure 7:** Graphic model representation

The user has selected the sector "Event Strategy" in the framework. The attributes of this sector can be viewed in the attribute window, which can be navigated though using a vertical scrollbar. In addition to the general attribute group and the attribute group on the model status, which can be seen in Figure 7, further attributes exist that characterize the model components such as, creator, date created, inspector, date of inspection, person responsible for release, date of release, validity period, etc.

## 6.3   Interaction Design with the Basis Modeling Tool

If the user wishes to carry out changes on a model-version he must first open the modeling tool. This can be done by clicking the button "Edit". This command opens the file assigned to the information model component marked on the "Graphic"-card. In Figure 7, the user has marked the component "Event Strategy" of the reference model framework "Event-E". Using the "Edit"-button he can open the process model assigned to "Event Strategy" in its current version. This "jump" to the modeling tool is represented in Figure 8. In addition to reading, changing or deleting models and model elements, the user can now use further functionalities of the modeling tool. This pertains for example, to the graphic arrangement and grouping of model elements, the creation of model elements and element attributes, the placing of attributes or the connection of a model with OLE-objects, such as for example, text documents or slides.

## 6.4  Managing Model Versions

The management of the model and model-element versions made in the course of a reference modeling project (model history) is carried out via the dialog reachable using the button "Versions" of the graphic index card (cf. Figure 8). In addition to the most important model data such as name, type or time of creation and modification, those responsible for the change, the type, reason, priority and status of the model changes, as well as the associated project activities are recorded.

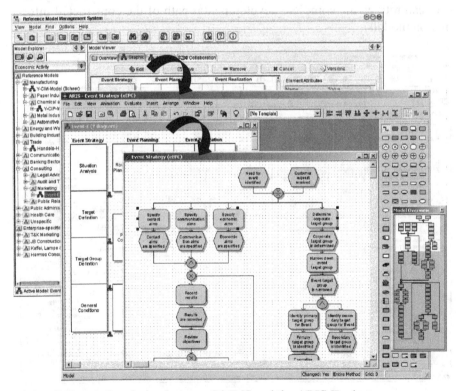

**Figure 8:** Interaction design between RMMS and the ARIS-Toolset

After pressing the button "Versions", the version management dialog opens for the model displayed in the "Graphic"-window resp. for the model element selected in the representation window. Figure 9 shows an open version management-dialog. The case represented here is, that the user "Johann Spuling" wishes to retrace the history of the model "Event Strategy" after confirming the adoption of the modifications he had made to the EPC-model "Event Strategy" (cf. Figure 8). For this purpose, he has opened the corresponding path in the model explorer and called up the "Version Graph"-dialog.

The graphic displayed in the dialog "Version Graph" in Figure 9 represents the structural relationships stored in the RMMS-database between the versions of the active EPC-model in the "Graphic"-window. The version graph can be navigated using the vertical and horizontal scrollbar. With a simple mouse-click, the user selects the version element-constructs. The attributes of the marked version element are displayed in the right side of the window ("Attributes"). By double-clicking, one can display the model assigned to the version construct in the "Graphic"-window. This way, the user can retrace the complete developmental path of the constructed information models.

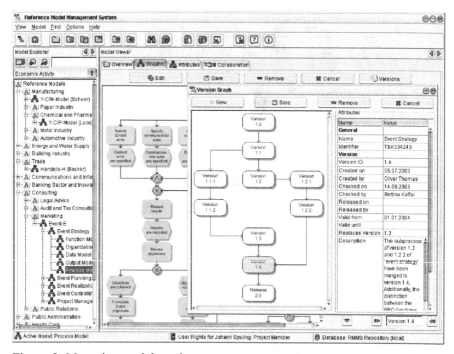

**Figure 9:** Managing model versions

Using the toolbar at the top of the "Version Graph"-window, the user can create new models or model-element versions ("New"), save attribute changes ("Save"), remove marked version constructs ("Remove") or reject respective changes and close the window ("Cancel"). The version numbers are automatically generated by the RMMS. They can however, be changed by the user at a later point in time.


# 7    Related Work

Within the framework of a study on method engineering GREIFFENBERG et al. introduced an approach for the configuration management of information models [EsGK02; Grei04]. On the basis of available standards, as well as the corresponding experience reports ("best practices") from software development, the authors systematized the requirements on a model versioning tool. The natural language depictions are represented by diagrams of the so-called $E^3$-method [Grei04, pp. 99 ff.] – and thus, transferred to a system specification for the versioning of information models. The concept was however, not implemented nor tested in practice. Which requirements are necessary for the integration of the approach in professional modeling tools was also not dealt with by the authors.

VOM BROCKE differentiates between new constructions, version constructions and variant constructions in his study on the design and distribution of construction processes according to the technical construction theory [Broc03, p. 260]. Furthermore, the author emphasizes the versioning of reference models and enterprise-specific models, on the basis of so-called reference model components, as noteworthy in comparison to "conventional" methods for the construction of reference models [Broc03, pp. 262 f.]. He relates this to the documentation of the evolution of a stock of models achievable with the version relationships between constructions in all levels of the construction process. However, he does not say how these relationships are to be fashioned.

WARNECKE et al. also allude, within the framework of an evolution concept for reference models, to the fact that "the increasing range of reference models, as well as the multitude of versions to be managed [...] complicate the use of a reference model" [WSHF98, p. 63] and state that "in addition [...] all versions of a reference model must be managed and available at any time" [WSHF98, p. 63]. The authors do not however, answer the questions as to how the versioning of information resp. reference models can be designed.

Further related work deals generally with the systematization of reference models, whereby it is, in fact, the tabulation of reference models that is meant here and not so much the survey-like textual description of the actual stock of reference models found in literature [FeLo02a, pp. 13 ff.;

FeLo02b, p. 15; FeLo03, pp. 46 f.; KlWi98, pp. 30 f.; Lang97, pp. 21 ff.; Mert92, pp. 20 ff.; Scho90, pp. 131 ff.]. It is indisputable that a model management, based on the cataloging of reference models, is very useful for the developers and users of reference models. It systematizes and facilitates access to the models and is suitable for supporting the search and selection of reference models. The said form for the model management is however based, as a rule, on the assumption of a given stock of models. Which advanced requirements must be made to model management when the changes in a model over time (model evolution) are also to be considered, is not dealt with in the said studies.

## 8   Discussion of the Results and Outlook

Procedure models for reference modeling predominantly give recommendations for an incremental construction, i. e. the creation of a model step by step, whereby the development of the model progresses with each step – they are quasi constructed as a sequence of "increments". Despite this connection, few studies exist, which deal with the problem of model versioning connected with this incremental development of reference models. The article at hand has accommodated this fact by designing an information system, which supports the version management of reference models. The illustrated approach corresponds to an evolution concept for reference models in which know-how from previous modeling tasks can be "conserved" in order to make it available within the framework of other problems or tasks. The concept was designed on the basis of data structures and a system architecture and implemented in the form of an application system.

It became clear in the design phase that the creative potential in the revisional management and control of the development and usage of reference models is justified from the perspective of a basic information model-term, as well as from the perspective of a specific reference model-term. Due to the use-oriented understanding of reference models in this article, as well as the generally heterogeneous stock of models, the formation of the concept and data structures had to be geared toward the versioning of information models, instead of solely to reference models. Based on this, the version management could be designed as a function whose performance in modeling projects is *first*, permanently carried out, *second*, serves the evolution of the results to be produced in these projects (information and reference models) and *third*, supports the development, as well as the usage of reference models.

The central thoughts in the prototypical implementation were *first*, the implementation of the versioning as an "integrating" component in a professional modeling tool and *second*, the use of version graphs taken from the field of software engineering. It is especially these graphs, which form a basis for the navigation of model-versions, enriched thanks to their graphic representations. The result is a prototype, which allows system-users to retrace model histories.

It must however, be criticized that the existing relationships between the information models and model-elements resp. information model-versions and element versions used, are ultimately a simplified interpretation of the relationships existing between a model and the elements of a model. They provide no information as to how model-elements resp. element versions are to be aggregated to form a model resp. model-version. The author sees a future challenge in the extension of the approach to the construction techniques currently discussed in the field of reference modeling, as well as in the embedding of other forms of version graphs, such as for example, sequences, trees and acyclic graphs.

## Acknowledgements

The system presented in this article was developed at the Institute for Information Systems (IWi) at the German Research Center for Artificial Intelligence (DFKI) in Saarbruecken. The development of the system was funded by the "Deutsche Forschungsgemeinschaft" (German Research Foundation) within the research project "Reference Model-Based Customizing with Vague Data" as part of the initiative BRID[2]. The author is grateful to Johann Spuling for supporting the implementation of the presented prototype.

## References

[ABCM99] Asklund, U.; Bendix, L.; Christensen, H. B.; Magnusson, B.: The Unified Extensional Versioning Model. In: Estublier, J. (ed.): System configuration management: 9th international symposium; SCM–9. Toulouse, September 5-7, 1999. Berlin et al. 1999, pp. 100-122

[Balz98] Balzert, H.: Lehrbuch der Software-Technik: Software-Management, Software-Qualitätssicherung, Unternehmensmodellierung. Heidelberg 1998.

[BDKK02] Becker, J.; Delfmann, P.; Knackstedt, R.; Kuropka, D.: Konfigurative Referenzmodellierung. In: Becker, J.; Knackstedt, R. (eds.): Wissensmanagement mit Referenzmodellen: Konzepte für die Anwendungssystem- und Organisationsgestaltung. Heidelberg 2002, pp. 25-144.

[BeDK02] Becker, J.; Delfmann, P.; Knackstedt, R.: Eine Modellierungstechnik für die konfigurative Referenzmodellierung. In: Becker, J.; Knackstedt, R. (eds.): Referenzmodellierung 2002: Methoden – Modelle – Erfahrungen. Münster 2002, pp. 35-79.

[BeDK04] Becker, J.; Delfmann, P.; Knackstedt, R.: Adaption fachkonzeptioneller Referenzprozessmodelle. Industrie Management 20 (2004) 1, pp. 19-22.

[BeHS80] Bersoff, E. H.; Henderson, V. D.; Siegel, S. G.: Software configuration management: An investment in product integrity. Englewood Cliffs 1980.

[BrBu04] vom Brocke, J.; Buddendick, C.: Konstruktionstechniken für die Referenzmodellierung – Systematisierung, Sprachgestaltung und Werkzeugunterstützung. In: Becker, J.; Delfmann, P. (eds.): Referenzmodellierung: Grundlagen, Techniken und domänenbezogene Anwendung. Heidelberg 2004, pp. 19-49.

[Broc03] vom Brocke, J.: Referenzmodellierung: Gestaltung und Verteilung von Konstruktionsprozessen. Berlin 2003.

[CoWe98] Conradi, R.; Westfechtel, B.: Version models for software configuration management. ACM Computing Surveys 30 (1998). 2, pp. 232-282.

[EsCa95] Estublier, J.; Casallas, R.: Three Dimensional Versioning. In: Estublier, J. (ed.): Software Configuration Management, ICSE SCM– 4 and SCM–5 Workshops, Selected Papers. London 1995, pp. 118-135.

[EsGK02] Esswein, W.; Greiffenberg, S.; Kluge, C.: Konfigurationsmanagement von Modellen. In: Sinz, E. J.; Plaha, M. (eds.): Modellierung betrieblicher Informationssysteme: MobIS 2002; Proceedings der Tagung MobIS 2002 im Rahmen der Multi-Konferenz Wirtschaftsinformatik (MKWI 2002) vom 9. bis 11. September 2002 in Nürnberg. Bonn 2002, pp. 93-112.

[Estu00] Estublier, J.: Software Configuration Management: A Road Map. In: Finkelstein, A. (ed.): The future of software engineering 2000: part of the 22nd International Conference on Software Engineering. New York 2000, pp. 279-289.

[FeLo02a] Fettke, P.; Loos, P.: Der Referenzmodellkatalog als Instrument des Wissensmanagements: Methodik und Anwendung. In: Becker, J.; Knackstedt, R. (eds.): Wissensmanagement mit Referenzmodellen: Konzepte für die Anwendungssystem- und Organisationsgestaltung. Heidelberg 2002, pp. 3-24.

[FeLo02b] Fettke, P.; Loos, P.: Klassifikation von Informationsmodellen – Nutzenpotentiale, Methode und Anwendung am Beispiel von Referenzmodellen. In: Loos, P. (ed.): Working Papers of the Research Group Information Systems & Management, no. 9, Johannes Gutenberg-University Mainz, 2002 (in German)

[FeLo02c] Fettke, P.; Loos, P.: Methoden zur Wiederverwendung von Referenzmodellen – Übersicht und Taxonomie. In: Becker, J.; Knackstedt, R. (eds.): Referenzmodellierung 2002: Methoden – Modelle – Erfahrungen. Münster 2002, pp. 9-33.

[FeLo03] Fettke, P.; Loos, P.: Classification of Reference Models – A Methodology and its Application. Information Systems and e-Business Management 1 (2003) 1, pp. 35-53.

[FeLo04] Fettke, P.; Loos, P.: Referenzmodellierungsforschung. Wirtschaftsinformatik 46 (2004) 5, pp. 331-340.

[Grei04] Greiffenberg, S.: Methodenentwicklung in Wirtschaft und Verwaltung. Hamburg 2004.

[Hars94] Hars, A.: Referenzdatenmodelle: Grundlagen effizienter Datenmodellierung. Wiesbaden 1994.

[IDS03] IDS Scheer AG (ed.): ARIS 6 – Collaborative Suite™, Version 6.1. White Paper, March 2003. Saarbrücken 2003.

[IDS05] IDS Scheer AG (ed.): Meilensteine in der Unternehmensgeschichte. http://www.ids-scheer.de/international/german/investor/milestones. 2005.

[KlWi98] Klabunde, S.; Wittmann, M.: Referenzmodelle und -bibliotheken: Ein Thesenpapier im Rahmen des Forschungsverbundprojektes "Geschäftsprozeßgestaltung mit integrierten Prozeß- und Produktmodellen". Saarbrücken 1998.

[Lang97] Lang, K.: Gestaltung von Geschäftsprozessen mit Referenzprozeßbausteinen. Wiesbaden 1997.

[MeHo75] Mertens, P.; Holzner, J.: Eine Gegenüberstellung von Integrationsansätzen der Wirtschaftsinformatik. Wirtschaftsinformatik 34 (1992) 1, pp. 5-25.

[MeNü03] Mendling, J.; Nüttgens, M.: XML-basierte Geschäftsprozessmodellierung. In: Uhr, W.; Esswein, W.; Schoop, E. (eds.): Wirtschaftsinformatik 2003: Medien – Märkte – Mobilität; Band 2. Heidelberg 2003, pp. 161-180.

[Roch75] Rochkind, M. J.: The Source Code Control System. IEEE Transactions on Software Engineering 1 (1975) 4, pp. 364-370.

[Sche02] Scheer, A.-W.: ARIS – Vom Geschäftsprozess zum Anwendungssystem. 4th edition, Berlin et al. 2002.

[Sche90] Scheer, A.-W.: EDV-orientierte Betriebswirtschaftslehre: Grundlagen für ein effizientes Informationsmanagement. 4th edition, Berlin et al. 1990.

[Sche97] Scheer, A.-W.: Wirtschaftsinformatik: Referenzmodelle für industrielle Geschäftsprozesse. 7th edition, Berlin et al. 1997.

[Schl00] Schlagheck, B.: Objektorientierte Referenzmodelle für das Prozess- und Projektcontrolling: Grundlagen – Konstruktion – Anwendungsmöglichkeiten. Wiesbaden 2000.

[Scho00] Scholz-Reiter, B.: CIM – Informations- und Kommunikationssysteme: Darstellung von Methoden und Konzeption eines rechnergestützten Werkzeugs für die Planung. Munich 1990.

[Schü98] Schütte, R.: Grundsätze ordnungsmäßiger Referenzmodellierung: Konstruktion konfigurations- und anpassungsorientierter Modelle. Wiesbaden 1998.

[Schw99] Schwegmann, A.: Objektorientierte Referenzmodellierung: Theoretische Grundlagen und praktische Anwendung. Wiesbaden 1999.

[Sinu04] Sinur, J.: Magic Quadrant for Business Process Analysis, 2004. Stamford, CT: Gartner Research, 2004. Gartner's Application Development & Maintenance Research Note M–22–0651, 4 March 2004.

[Somm01] Sommerville, I.: Software Engineering. 6th edition, Munich 2001.

[Stac73] Stachowiak, H.: Allgemeine Modelltheorie. Vienna 1973.

[ThAH03] Thomas, O.; Adam, O.; Herrmann, K.: Adaption von Referenzmodellen unter Berücksichtigung unscharfer Daten. In: Dittrich, K.; König, W.; Oberweis, A.; Rannenberg, K.; Wahlster, W. (eds.): Informatik 2003 – Innovative Informatikanwendungen: Band 1. Bonn 2003, pp. 243-248.

[ThAS05] Thomas, O.; Adam, O.; Seel, C.: Business Process Management with Vague Data. In: Proceedings: DEXA 2005: 16th International Workshop on Database and Expert Systems Applications; 22–26 August 2005, Copenhagen, Denmark. Los Alamitos 2005, pp. 962-966.

[ThKL05] Thomas, O.; Kaffai, B.; Loos, P.: Referenzmodellbasiertes Event-Management mit Ereignisgesteuerten Prozessketten. In: Nüttgens, M.; Rump, F. J. (eds.): EPK 2005: Geschäftsprozessmanagement mit Ereignisgesteuerten Prozessketten; 4. Workshop der Gesellschaft für Informatik e.V. (GI) und Treffen ihres Arbeitskreises "Geschäftsprozessmanagement mit Ereignisgesteuerten Prozessketten (WI-EPK)". 08.-09. Dezember 2005 in Hamburg. Bonn 2005, pp. 74 -96.

[Thom05a] Thomas, O.: Das Modellverständnis in der Wirtschaftsinformatik: Historie, Literaturanalyse und Begriffsexplikation. In: Scheer, A.-W. (ed.): Veröffentlichungen des Instituts für Wirtschaftsinformatik, no. 183, Saarbrücken 2005.

[Thom05b] Thomas, O.: Understanding the Term Reference Model in Information Systems Research: History, Literature Analysis and Explanation. In: Kindler, E.; Nüttgens, M. (eds.): Business Process Reference Models: Proceedings of the Workshop on Business Process Reference Models (BPRM 2005); Salellite workshop of the 3rd International Conference on Business Process Management (BPM). Nancy, September 5, 2005. Nancy 2005, pp. 16-29.

[ThSc06] Thomas, O.; Scheer, A.-W.: Tool Support for the Collaborative Design of Reference Models – A Business Engineering Perspective. In: Proceedings of the 39th Annual Hawaii International Conference on System Sciences (HICSS'06), January 4 –7, 2006, Hyatt Regency Kauai, Poipu, Kauai, Hawaii. Accepted for presentation at the Minitrack "Collaboration Support for Integrated Modeling and Simulation".

[WSHF98] Warnecke, G.; Stammwitz, G.; Hallfell, F.; Förster, H.: Evolutionskonzept für Referenzmodelle. Industrie Management 14 (1998) 2, pp. 60-64.

[Zell97] Zeller, A.: Configuration Management with Version Sets: A Unified Software Versioning Model and its Applications. Braunschweig 1997.

# Adaptive Reference Modeling: Integrating Configurative and Generic Adaptation Techniques for Information Models

Jörg Becker, Patrick Delfmann, Ralf Knackstedt

**Abstract:** *Reference models have to be adapted to fit to the according application situation. In order to reduce the adaptation efforts, the concept of configurative reference modeling represents a promising approach. Nevertheless, since not every requirement of possible reference model users can be anticipated by the reference model developer, further model adaptations have to be performed. In order to support the reference model user decreasing his adaptation efforts by providing a higher methodological support, we propose to integrate generic model adaptation techniques with configurative reference modeling. Our paper presents recommendations for the construction of modeling languages that realize an integration of configurative and generic reference modeling.*

## 1 Introduction, Related Work, and Research Goal

### 1.1 Introduction

The development of information models is often an expensive and time consuming task. Consequently, approaches are required which increase the efficiency of information modeling. Against this background, reference models provide a useful means of reducing the effort of information modeling. Reference models are information models that are developed with the goal of being reused for different, but similar purposes. Furthermore, reference models are used as a starting point for the construction of project-specific models [Fran99; Rose03], e. g. in the course of business reengineering projects. The benefit of the use of reference models is predominantly the reduction of development costs, due to the possible reuse of knowledge. Furthermore, reference models are referred to as providing best or common practice solutions for information modeling projects [Silv01; RoAa07].

Nevertheless, reference models provide benefits only if the reduced modeling effort resulting through their reuse is not overlapped by the adaptation effort. Adaptations are necessary since the reference model has to comply with the particular application context. Application contexts depend on company specifics on the one hand and requirements of different user groups within a company on the other hand. This is why they can be divided into

- *Business characteristics and their values*: These describe the class of organization the reference model adaptation is to be accomplished for [WMBK03]. Examples for business characteristics of the domain of trade are *transaction type* or *distribution channel*. Exemplary forms of transaction types are *warehousing*, *third-party-deal* and *central settlement*.
- *Perspectives*: These represent the requirements of different user groups applying the information model [DaSh96; NJJZ96; Rose98; RoGr00]. They are determined by the pursued modeling intention, e. g. *software engineering* or *business process change*, the user's organizational role within the project, e. g. *method expert* or *user*, and further influence factors like the user's preferences regarding the *model layout* or used terms [BDKK02].

Considering both types of characteristics in the process of reference model adaptation a specific adaptation parameter structure results which is shown in Figure 1 as Entity-Relationship-Model [Chen76].

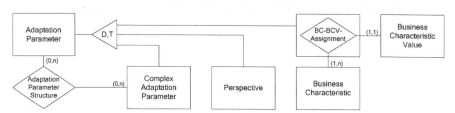

**Figure 1:** Adaptation parameter structure

In order to comply with particular application contexts, reference models are either to be aligned to a specific user group or need to comprise concepts that facilitate an easy and efficient adaptation process. Furthermore, the development of reference models is often costly, risky, and extensive. This moreover underlines the demand for an easy-to-use adaptation approach. Like every other entrepreneur, reference model developers need to identify their market potentials and their profits are subject to the product acceptance on the part of the customer (here companies and organizations). Thus, reference model developers face the following dilemma:

On the one hand, customers will choose a reference model that – alongside the quality of the transferred know-how – provides the best fit to their individual requirements and therefore implies the least need for changes.

On the other hand, a restriction of the generality of the model results in higher turn-over risks because of smaller sales markets.

## 1.2  Related Work, Research Problem, and Goal

Adaptive reference models provide a way out of this "reference modeling dilemma". They comprise rules which allow automatic modifications of the original reference model depending on company or project specific issues. In order to enable a context-specific adaptation of reference models, few conceptual modeling approaches have been developed in the near past:

SOFFER ET AL. propose configurable reference models in order to customize enterprise systems. They use configurable, so-called Object-Process Diagrams that integrate process flows and data objects used within an enterprise system. The configuration of these Diagrams is performed by interpreting attributes that define the relation of diagram objects to different application scenarios. During enterprise systems customizing, the users have to specify their application context. Based on this, the attributes are interpreted, and the models are modified accordingly [SoGD03].

ROSEMANN & VAN DER AALST propose a configurable reference modeling language that is based on Event Driven Process Chains (EPC). The approach differs from that of SOFFER ET AL. in so far as configurations are less predefined. It is based on semantic patterns in process models that describe dependencies of model elements on a semantic basis. E. g., a manual model configuration step that erases a process branch is followed by a hint to erase another process branch as well that is semantically related to the prior one. Similarly to SOFFER ET AL., the authors point out the necessity to connect model elements to the according enterprise systems functions in order to perform model and enterprise systems configuration concurrently [RoAa07].

The approach which has been introduced by BECKER ET AL. is based on the view building Architecture of Integrated Information Systems" (ARIS [Sche00]) in order to comply with different modeling views that are needed for the integrated modeling of information systems and business processes. In comparison to the approaches of SOFFER ET AL. as well as ROSEMANN & VAN DER AALST, it is different inasmuch several configuration mechanisms are provided that have different influences on the models. The configuration mechanisms are able to format modeling languages, models, model sections and model elements in order to fit the model base to context specific requirements. Furthermore, the approach is not restricted to conceptual configurations. It allows also modifications of the graphical representation of models as well as the management of different languages and language-internal synonyms.

The configuration strategy of each of the introduced approaches is similar. Model variants for different application scenarios are integrated in one model and are predefined. The model variant that is considered the best for a specific application scenario can be selected. Therefore, these approaches provide a useful means of reducing the efforts for reference model adaptation, since the adaptation of reference models to different purposes is supported methodically.

The configuration approaches can be used in different stages of reference model adaptation as Figure 2 shows. First, reference models have to be adapted to the according enterprise (here: a retail enterprise that only performs warehousing; furthermore, enterprise employees demand overview models instead of detail models). Second, they are configured company-internally in order to comply with the requirements of different user groups (here: a project team that includes only practitioners, why the models have to be made easy-to-read). Third, a further configuration step is imaginable that adapts the model base to requirements of single users, e. g. employees of distribution. Hence, the configuration process can be performed repeatedly in order to support the adaptation process in each stage.

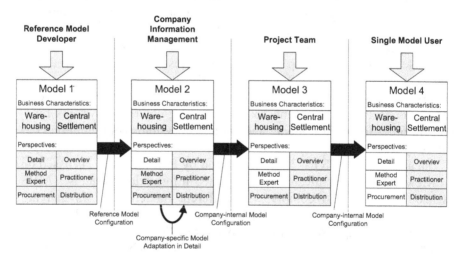

**Figure 2:** Exemplary, multi-level configuration process [BKKD01]

Since a reference model developer is not able to anticipate every possible specific of a company, the reference model that is adapted to a specific business characteristic in the first stage, has to be fine-adapted to company specifics in a second stage, before it can be configured to fit the requirements of company-internal user groups. This fine-adaptation causes further adaptation costs. Consequently, a methodical support of the reference model user should be available in order to decrease these additional costs. This is ignored by common configuration approaches.

At this stage, generic modeling approaches, e. g. generic component driven approaches, are considered appropriate, since they offer less predefined reusable model fragments. This way, on the one hand, the modeling "freedom" is assured. On the other hand, the modeler is supported by methodical concepts that promise an acceleration of the fine-adaptation process. Approaches to generic information modeling can be found e. g. in [Risi00; FeYu00; Szyp02; Kilo91].

Nevertheless, each of these approaches is isolated. An integrated approach to adaptive reference modeling that comprises configurative and generic adaptation concepts is still missing. Hence, in order to close this gap, we propose an integrated approach based on the configurative reference modeling approach of BECKER ET AL. in this contribution. Therefore we first introduce our research methodology and our paradigmatic positioning very briefly in section 2. The framework and basic conceptual specifications are topic of section 3. In section 4, we present configurative adaptation mechanisms for reference models that are integrated with generic adaptation mechanisms in section 5. The conceptual specifications of section 4 and 5 are illustrated with a running example based on Event-Driven Process Chains (EPC) [Sche00]. The paper concludes with section 6, where we discuss efficiency aspects of the proposed modeling approach as well as necessary further research.

## 2 Research Methodology

In terms of research methodology, we follow WEICK'S sensemaking paradigm [Weic95]. The relevance of the research topic was derived from requirements the authors were confronted with during information model-driven consulting projects. These were performed amongst others in the companies *Deutsche Telekom AG* [BeKR03] and *Bayer Business Services GmbH* [BJDF06], in *public administrations in the north-west of Germany* [BADN03] and in the *German Ministry of Defense*. The requirements gathered within these consulting projects were balanced with already existing approaches to information model adaptation as briefly outlined in section 1.2, whereas a deficit of methodical support for this problem was identified.

A second sensemaking aspect of the research project is that modeling languages were selected as a basis for the specification of adaptation support which are well-known, well-established and wide-spread. Furthermore, these modeling languages are provided by a modeling tool distributed by the market leader in terms of conceptual modeling. Therefore, the modeling languages we apply in our approach are based on the *Architecture of Integrated Information Systems (ARIS)* [Sche00]. Hereby, we expect a quick dissemination and application of our findings.

The construction part of the research is interpretivist in nature [KlMy99] with respect to processing the empirical material (mainly conceptual models) that the authors were provided from their industry partners.

## 3    A Framework for Adaptation Support

### 3.1  Dimensions

With the aim of structuring the specification of adaptation support for reference models, a framework is applied that is spanned by three dimensions (cf. Figure 3).

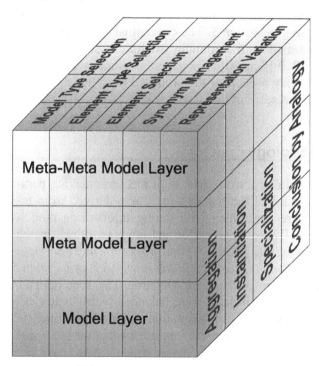

**Figure 3:** Framework [BeDK04]

In order to specify the adaptation concepts, we make use of meta modeling. Meta models are used to specify modeling languages [Stra96;
NJJZ96]. Within the *first dimension* of the framework, we distinguish the
*model layer*, the *meta model layer* and the *meta-meta model layer*. The
model layer is used to present adaptation examples that are based on EPCs.
On meta model layer, we specify the language of EPCs exemplarily and
show modifications that are performed within this language in the course
of the adaptation process. The adaptation mechanisms themselves are
specified on meta-meta model layer. The specification on meta-meta
model layer is necessary because, on the one hand, this way, adaptation
mechanisms are possible that are able to adapt modeling languages. On the
other hand, through this, the adaptation concepts can be reused for other
modeling languages specified on meta model layer, e. g. Entity-Relationship Models, Organigrams, Technical Term Models etc. As specification
language on meta model layer as well as on meta-meta model layer, we
use Entity-Relationship-Models [Chen76] with (min, max)-cardinalities.

The *second dimension* differentiates five categories of *configuration
mechanisms* which in part have single mechanisms assigned. The configuration is characterized by explicit adaptation points enclosed in the reference model. For these adaptation points rules are defined that determine
how the reference model is to be modified [BDKK02; BDDK04]. The configuration is dependent on the current value of the configuration parameter.
In the course of configuration specific models are derived from the reference model.

The fundamental concept of configurative reference model adaptation is
based upon the principle of *model projection*. I. e., starting from a total
model that contains information for each application context, model sections are faded out that are not relevant for a specific application context.
The fading out is realized by configuration mechanisms which use adaptation parameters as input [BDKK02].

So as to support the reference modeler by model projection efficiently, it
is beneficial to supply configuration mechanisms that have different impacts on the models. Therefore, configuration mechanisms are not exclusively proposed for the layer of modeling technique application (model
layer), but also for the layer of their definition (meta model layer). Configurative adaptations of meta-models act upon on all models which were
constructed in the corresponding modeling language, whereas adaptations
on model layer only act upon specific models and model sections respectively. We distinguish the following configuration mechanisms:

- *Model Type Selection* allows for providing only those modeling languages and their according model types to users that are relevant for

them. E. g., employees who use process models as guidelines for their everyday work, do not need to be provided with data models describing data base structures.

- *Element Type Selection* considers the necessity to provide modeling language variants with different expressive power for different user groups. E. g., practitioners prefer process models that are easy to read. This can be achieved by e. g. fading out resource types that are annotated to process functions.

- In contrast to Model Type and Element Type Selection, the configuration mechanism of *Element Selection* does not operate on the according modeling language but on particular parts of a model. E. g., process branches which are not relevant for a certain type of business can be faded out. We distinguish Term-based Element Selection and Attribute-based Element Selection. Term-based Element Selection assigns logical terms to model elements that connect them directly to perspectives or business characteristics, whereupon Attribute-based Element Selection assigns characteristics to model elements that mark them as relevant or non-relevant for different perspectives or business characteristics. The differentiation of these mechanisms was undertaken in order to support the reference model developer efficiently in different adaptation scenarios.

- In different parts of a company different naming conventions may have established, whereas the different namings have the same meaning (E. g., procurement employees call a supplier invoice just "invoice", whereas distribution employees use the naming "supplier invoice"). In order to consider these conventions in line with information modeling, the configuration mechanism of *Synonym Management* allows for perspective-specific exchanging of model element namings.

- Through *Representation Variation*, the representational aspect of modeling languages can be changed dependent on the current perspective. I. e., symbols of model elements can be exchanged (for further representational variations of models cf. [BDKK02]).

The *third dimension* distinguishes four types of *generic reference model adaptation mechanisms*. Unlike configuration mechanisms, they allow creative freedom within the adaptation process. The possible model variants are less predefined.

- *Aggregation* implies that the reference model is provided in the form of model components that have to be combined by the reference model user. [Szyp02; Kilo91; HaPS99]. The possible combinations of components can thereby be restricted by interface definitions.

- The *Instantiation* of a reference model envisions the insertion of feasible values for placeholders that are provided within the model [Broc03; BeDK04]. These values can reach from simple numeric values to complex model element structures.
- In many cases the adaptation of a reference model by *Specialization* is envisioned. In this case the level of detail of the reference model is consciously restricted. Specialization is performed by adding, changing or removing model elements without any semantic restrictions.
- Finally, the reuse of model structures found in a reference model by the user is referred to as *Conclusion by Analogy* [Broc03], which is the fewest restricted adaptation mechanism.

It is reasonable to combine different generic adaptation mechanisms. E. g. components that can be instantiated provide a higher degree of reusability. Compositions of design patterns pursue this strategy [Risi00; FeYu00].

In the following, we will use the framework as a navigator in order to illustrate conceptual specifications as belonging to an according section of the framework. E. g., basic specifications of the meta-meta model layer are marked by hatching the whole upper layer of the framework. An example that shows how an EPC on model layer is modified by Element Selection is indicated by shading the lower middle cell in the front of the framework. Specifications that describe a combination of Aggregation and Representation Variation on meta model layer are indicated by shading the front, vertically middle and horizontally right sub-cube of the framework.

The specifications of the adaptation mechanisms that are presented in detail in the sections 4 and 5 are based on constitutional specifications on different model layers that we introduce in the following.

## 3.2  Constitutional Specifications

The central construct of the meta-meta model level is the *element type*, by means of which the existence of model elements on meta model layer is defined. Since for the meta model layer Entity-Relationship-Models are applied as well, model elements on that layer are entity types and relationship types that are subsumed within the entity type *type* on meta-meta model layer (cf. for the complete specification [BDKK02]). Types have *attributes* and can be provided with *constraints* that facilitate restrictions for the instances of the associated types (cf. Figure 4).

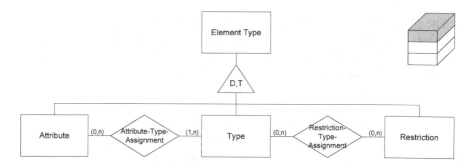

**Figure 4:** Constitutional specifications on meta-meta model layer

The assignment of attributes to types on meta model layer requires that each model element of a type (e. g. process functions) receives this attribute once it is defined. If individual instances of a type on model level require additional attributes, an extension of the meta model is necessary (cf. Figure 5).

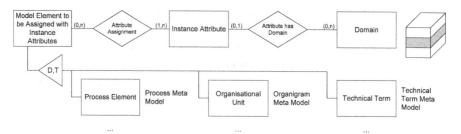

**Figure 5:** Instance attributes as constitutional specifications on meta model layer

All meta model elements that have to be provided with such an instance-based assignment are generalized within the entity type *model element to be assigned with instance attributes*. The *instance attribute* which in turn belongs to a certain *domain* (range of values) is assigned to this model element. The specialized meta model elements emanate from parts of the whole meta model which contain the specifications of different model types (e. g. EPCs, Organigrams etc.).

E. g. the entity type *process element* belongs to that part of the meta model that specifies the language of process models (cf. in detail [BDKK02). In the following, we will use the process meta model exemplarily and representatively for further modeling languages of other information system views. It is closely related to the EPC [KeNS92; Sche00]. In order to simplify the understanding of further language specifications, it is necessary to introduce the basic modeling language elements of the EPC (cf. Figure 6).

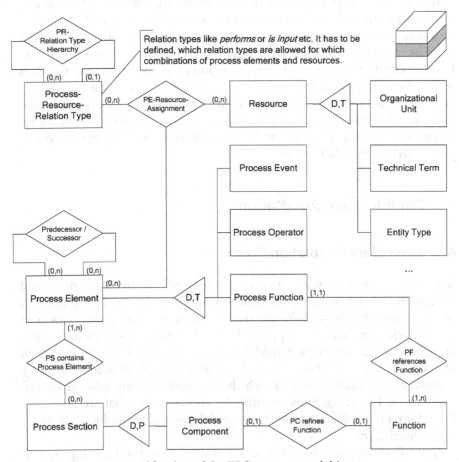

**Figure 6:** Language specification of the EPC on meta model layer

*Process functions* are always explicitly associated with one *function*. The construct of a function is introduced to facilitate the reuse of semantically identical activities in different processes without having to transfer process-specific dependencies. The assignment of process functions (pf) to functions is built through the relationship type *pf references function* between the entity types *function* and *process function*. Functions may build hierarchies, i. e. they can be refined through a complete *process component (pc)*. Process components are *process sections* which in turn have assigned *process elements (pe)* that are fundamental for EPCs (cf. entity type *process component* and relationship types *pc refines function* as well as *ps contains process element*).

If required, *resources* are assigned to process elements. All those elements that support the course of the process are subsumed via the resource. Resources can be e. g. *organizational units, technical terms, entity types,* etc. The relations between process elements and resources can vary. Therefore the entity type *process-resource-relation type* is introduced which is related to itself in order to enable the construction of a relation type hierarchy. The relationship type *pe-resource-assignment* describes specific relations between resources and process elements built through the ternary relationship type between the entity types *process element, resource* and *process-resource-relation type.*


## 4    Configurative Adaptation


### 4.1   Exemplary Adaptation Process

In the following, we show a running example which presents a simplified process model of invoice auditing in a retailing company. This process is adapted successively to different requirements, whereas each introduced configuration mechanism is applied. For each configuration, modifications either within the underlying modeling language specifications or within their instances are necessary. Thus, the model example is accompanied by a meta model example within which the modifications take place (cf. overview in Figure 7). Subsequently, the specifications that are necessary to perform the modifications on meta model layer, are introduced on meta-meta model layer.

In the first step, the process model is adapted to a specific company that performs two types of transaction simultaneously (warehousing & third-party-deal; cf. Figure 8). As a consequence, process branches that only serve the transaction type of central settlement are faded out. For this purpose, *Term-based Element Selection* is applied. E. g. the term that is annotated to the most right process branch "NOT TT (3PD | WH | (3PD | WH))" assigns this branch to all transaction types except third-party-deal (3PD), warehousing (WH) or a combination of both. I. e., it is visible only if central settlement is performed exclusively or in combination with the other transaction types. The configuration shows that this branch is faded out (1→2).

The following configuration steps consider company-internal requirements (cf. Figure 9). In a second configuration step, the process model is

adapted in order to produce an overview of the process that reduces the model to an EPC without annotated resources. This is e. g. relevant for consolidation meetings within distributed modeling environments. The configuration mechanism of *Element Type Selection* is applied that fades out the resource types *data* and *job* (2→3).

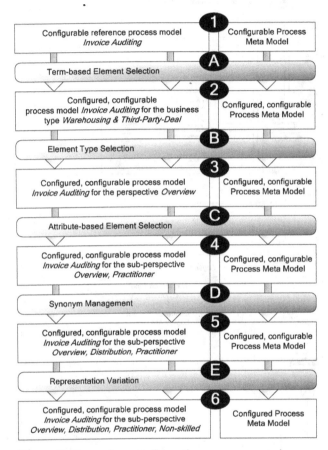

**Figure 7:** Exemplary configuration process overview

In a third step, the process model is adapted to requirements of practitioners that could be confused by the special syntax of the EPC that claims a strict alternating of functions and events. Semantically, not all events are necessary, since they just mark the successful termination of a function and do not provide further information concerning the following process flow. These "trivial" events are faded out by the configuration mechanism of *Attribute-based Element Selection*. Every event is assigned an attribute "trivial". If its value is TRUE, it is faded out (3→4).

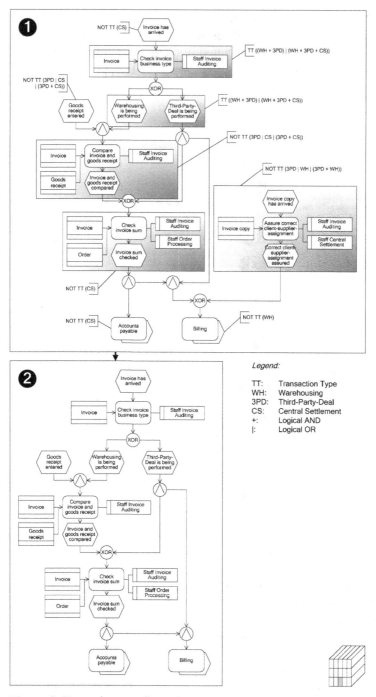

**Figure 8:** Exemplary configuration process – part 1

The fourth configuration step considers different naming conventions. If the process model is to be provided to employees of distribution, the denotation "invoice" may be misinterpreted as "client invoice", whereas "supplier invoice" is meant here. Thus, every occurrence of "invoice" is exchanged by "supplier invoice" by the configuration mechanism of *Synonym Management* (4→5).

The last configuration step exchanges the "standard" symbols of the EPC by pictograms in order to serve the requirements of non-skilled users who often prefer a more "colorful" format of a model [Allw98] by applying the configuration mechanism of *Representation Variation* (5→6).

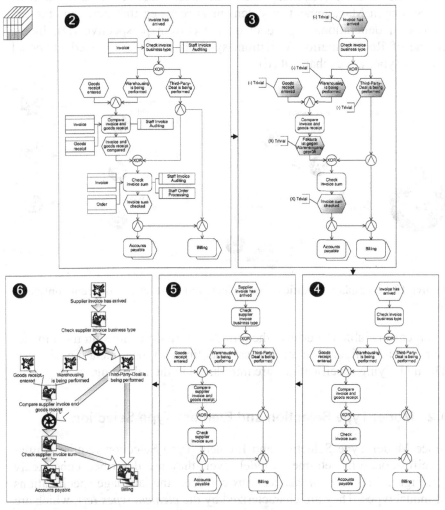

**Figure 9:** Exemplary configuration process – part 2

Figure 10 illustrates the modifications that are necessary on meta model layer in order to perform the configurations shown in the example. The Figure shows a section of the EPC meta model (cf. also Figure 6). In order to allow the first configuration step via Term-based Element Selection, an attribute has to exist that is able to contain the configuration terms (A). Element Type Selection that is performed in the second configuration step has to be able to fade out elements of the meta model hat represent element types on model layer (B). Attribute-based Element Selection applied in step three requires according attributes (cf. attribute "trivial") as well as a constraint that restricts the instances of the attributed model element type depending on the current adaptation parameter value (C). In order to realize Synonym Management, a statement is required that performs the exchange of denotations dependent on the current perspective (D). In the course of Representation Variation, symbols that are assigned to model element types are exchanged (E).

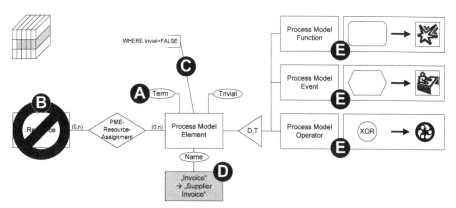

**Figure 10:** Exemplary modifications on meta model layer for different configuration steps

In order to be able to perform the introduced modifications on meta model layer, each configuration mechanism is defined on meta-meta model layer. The underlying specifications are introduced in the following.

## 4.2   Model Type Selection and Element Type Selection

Since Model Type Selection and Element Type Selection require similar specifications on meta-meta model layer, they are described concertedly (cf. Figure 11). *Meta model sections* comprise the language specifications of model types. They are characterized by the *element types (et)*, which are assigned to them, and their relations among each other. In case of the EPC, these are e. g. functions, events, and resources. A meta model section always contains the maximum number of allowed element types according to its model type. *Model type variants (mtv)* provide the basis for modifying model types. The model type variants are built by assigning element types to them which shall be faded out. The element types which are faded out per model type variant are noted in the *mtv-et-constriction*. Each model type variant is assigned to one or more *perspectives*. This way it is possible to hide complete model types for certain perspectives (Model Type Selection) or to vary the amount of applicable element types per model type and perspective (Element Type Selection).

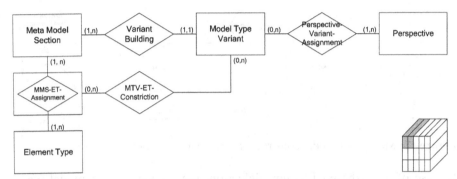

**Figure 11:** Meta-meta model constructs for Element Type Selection

Since the meta-meta model specifies the language of the meta model, instances of the entity type element type represent entity types or relationship types on meta model layer. If these instances are removed by creating according instances of the relationship type *mtv-et-constriction*, the corresponding meta model elements are no longer a part of the meta model (cf. configuration B in Figure 10). Model elements which are instances of a faded out meta model element are, in turn, faded out from the model layer.

## 4.3  Element Selection

Attribute-based Element Selection operates on the specifications of element types. In order to represent Element Selection, the existence of constraints for element types is defined (cf. entity type *declarative constraint* in Figure 12). These constraints are able to restrict the set of valid instances of element types. Further on, a constraint depends on the actual configuration. This is why it is assigned to the entity type *adaptation parameter* via the relationship type *attribute-based element selection* in the meta-meta model. An additional entity type *attribute for attribute-based element selection* as a specialization of the *attribute* in the meta-meta model is introduced. This specialization enables to define whether an attribute is valid for Element Selection or not. These specifications enable – dependent on the current adaptation parameter value – the annotation of a constraint to the according element type on meta model layer as it is exemplary shown in Figure 10 (C). As a consequence, each instance of an element type that is not selected by the constraint, is faded out.

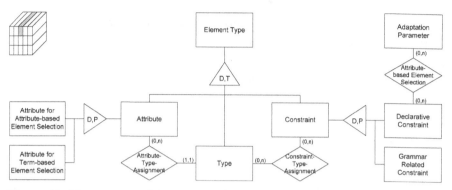

**Figure 12:** Meta-meta model constructs for Element Selection

In case of Term-based Element Selection, the relevance of a model element for a selected configuration depends on a logical term which is assigned to the element. In this context logical terms are understood as special attributes that can be assigned to model elements. They describe directly in which configuration the according model element is available. Terms have to comply with a predefined grammar (cf. Figure 13) for interpretation purposes. The grammar used here is based upon the extended Backus-Naur-Form (eBNF) [ISO96].

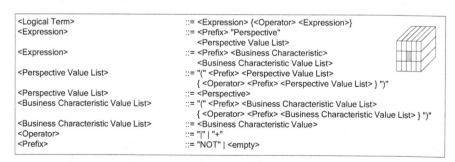

**Figure 13:** Grammar for term-based Element Selection

Term-based Element Selection is realized by introducing a special attribute type (cf. entity type *attribute* and its specialization *attribute for term-based element selection* in Figure 12) in the meta-meta model for types on meta model layer. In order to ensure the formal correctness of the logical terms it is necessary to define the existence of a further constraint that assures the specification of terms within attributes by using the introduced grammar (cf. the specialization *grammar related constraint* of the entity type *constraint*).

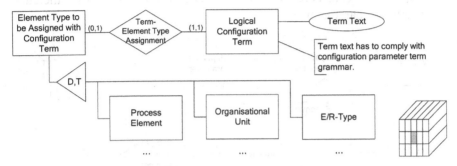

**Figure 14:** Meta model constructs for term-based Element Selection

In order to be able to assign logical configuration terms to every possible element type, it is necessary to add a language extension on meta model layer as well. For this purpose all element types from all modeling languages which support a term assignment are generalized within one element type (cf. Figure 14; for reasons of clarity it shows just a part of all model elements which are suitable for a term assignment). An element type which is suitable for a term assignment is related to the *logical configuration* term. This term holds an attribute which contains the *term text* and which belongs to the very type attribute for term-based Element Selection which was previously defined on meta-meta model layer (cf. also Figure 10 (A)). The constraint which is annotated to the term refers to the type *grammar related constraint* and ensures the formulation of the term text according to the introduced grammar. Evidently, the grammar related constraint which is defined on meta-meta model layer has got exactly one instance on meta model layer.

The result for the model layer is the following: Logical terms can be assigned to model elements which are instances of the meta model element element type to be assigned with configuration term. These can be evaluated by an appropriate interpreter. Subsequently, fade-outs can be performed according to the configuration parameter values which are defined within the terms (cf. example in Figure 8).

## 4.4  Synonym Management

The configuration mechanism of Synonym Management enables the exchange of model element denotations dependent on the current adaptation
parameter value. For such an amount of synonyms an according *wildcard*
is introduced in configurable reference models. Within the configuration
process, this wildcard is replaced with the adequate denotation for the current adaptation parameter value.

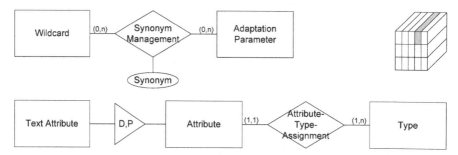

**Figure 15:** Meta-meta model constructs for Synonym Management

In the meta-meta model *adaptation parameters* are related to *wildcards*
(cf. Figure 15). Dependent on the adaptation parameter value, every wildcard instance is replaced by the according synonym that is stored in the attribute of the relationship type *synonym management*. E. g. the wildcard
"invoice" is replaced by the synonym "supplier invoice" if the perspective
"distribution" is active. Since the replacement of denotations should only
occur in attributes that contain text, Synonym Management operates exclusively on *text attributes* that are specified through the specialization *text
attribute* of the *attribute*. On meta model layer, these replacement rules are
explicated for every adaptation parameter value (e. g. "every occurrence of
'invoice' in text attributes shall be replaced by 'supplier invoice'"; cf. Figure 10 (D)).

## 4.5  Representation Variation

In order to realize Representation Variation, *element types* of *meta model
sections* are related to *symbols* and *perspectives* on meta-meta model layer
(cf. Figure 16). This means first, that element types that occur in different
model types can have different symbols in different model types. Second,
dependent on the perspective, the symbol of an element type of the same
model type can vary. On meta model layer, the symbols belonging to element types can be explicated as it is exemplary presented in Figure 10 (E).

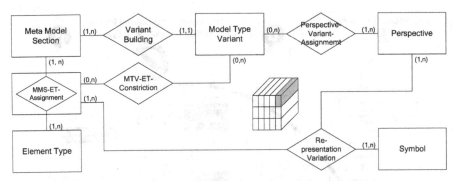

**Figure 16:** Meta-meta model constructs for Representation Variation

# 5   Integrating Generic Adaptation Mechanisms

Starting from problem of company-specific fine-adaptation that was already introduced in section 1.3, we will reuse the configuration example in the following in order to show how generic adaptation mechanisms can support the acceleration of the adaptation process.

## 5.1  Exemplary Adaptation Process

Once the process model is adapted to the company after the first configuration step (1→2, cf. Figure 17), some company-specific adaptations have to be performed that could not be anticipated by the reference model developer. In the example, the reference model user needs a stricter invoice sum check than it is provided by the reference model. A common check procedure is known as the principle of "second set of eyes", which could be stored within a repository as generic process component (α) and chosen by the reference model user. In order to fit this component to the configured reference model, it has to be concretized. First, the abstract denotations of the model elements are adapted to the application context "invoice auditing" (cf. grey shaded elements in Figure 17, (β)) which is realized by Instantiation. Second, missing elements like responsible organizational units have to be added. The appropriate elements can furthermore be found in the previously configured reference model by Conclusion by Analogy (cf. black shaded elements in Figure 17 (β)). Third, some elements both of the process component and the primary configured reference model have to be erased in order to fit in the component by Specialization (cf. crossed-out elements in Figure 17 (β & 2)).

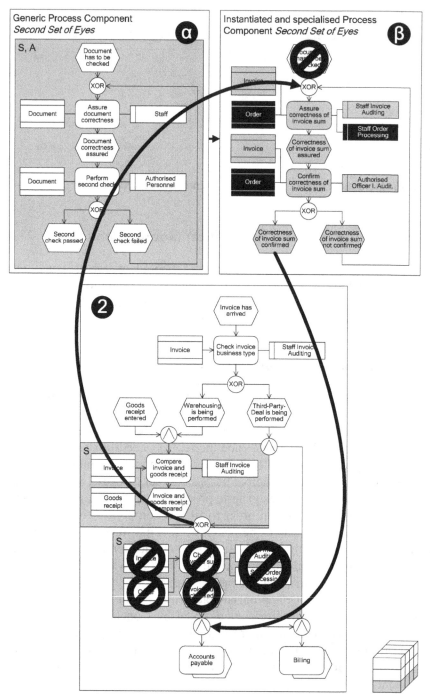

**Figure 17:** Generic adaptation step within the exemplary configuration process

Once the process model is conceptually adapted to the requirements of the company, it can be aggregated with the previously configured reference model (cf. bold arrows in Figure 17), and the configuration process outlined in section 4.1 can continue. Consequently, the parts of the reference model that have been modified, have to be enriched with configuration rules (cf. section 4).

In order to facilitate the combination of configurative and generic adaptation mechanisms it is reasonable to reuse the same concepts for the specification of generic adaptation mechanisms as for configuration mechanisms and to integrate them into the same framework. In the following, both reference model components and instantiated and specialized model parts as well as reference models created through Conclusion by Analogy are understood as parts of a universal model that shows only those parts that are relevant for the particular user. For a better understanding the generic adaptation mechanisms will first be introduced separately on the different model layers. Hence the dimension of configuration mechanisms will now be neglected when spanning the framework further on serving as the navigator.

## 5.2  Aggregation

Reference model components that are understood as part of a universal model can be specified on meta model layer as element types which equals an instance *component* of the entity type element type on meta-meta model layer (cf. table in Figure 18).

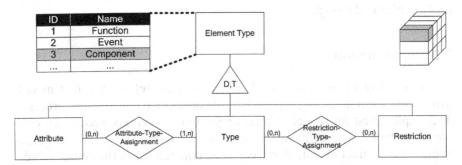

**Figure 18:** Meta-meta model constructs for Aggregation

The consideration of different model types leads to the definition of model type specific resp. view specific components on the one hand (cf. the specializations of the entity type *component* on meta model level in Figure 19) as well as to model type spanning resp. view spanning components on the other hand. The relationship type *component hierarchy* serves the latter by facilitating components that may contain components of different model types.

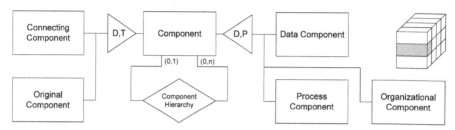

**Figure 19:** Meta model constructs for Aggregation

The aggregation of components of different model types is restricted through the syntax specifications of model type integration in partial models of the meta model layer (cf. exemplarily Figure 6).

E. g., a connection between a process component and a component of the resource view (data, organization, etc.) in the process meta model is built via instances of the relationship type *pe-resource-assignment*. In this context those components that have previously been constructed by the reference model constructor (*original component*) are distinguished from those that serve the user in connecting the selected original components (*connecting component*). In the easiest case the latter solely consist of one model element.

The application of Aggregation on model layer is shown in Figure 17. Once a component is chosen and concretized, it is connected to the previously configured model.

## 5.3  Instantiation

The possibility of instantiation of information models means that model aspects are formulated vaguely or left idle during the construction process. This applies first for model elements resp. model sections, second for element attributes. The reference model user therefore has to be informed about such abstract objects that have to be concretized in the course of adaptation.

For model element types adequate attributes have to be provided which contain such an advice. For this purpose an attribute type *marker "abstract element"* is introduced on meta-meta model layer which serves the labeling of model elements to be instantiated (cf. Figure 20).

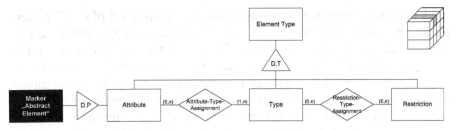

**Figure 20:** Meta-meta model constructs for Instantiation

Abstract attributes of model elements have to be designated analogically. These may differ dependent on the element on model. This is why *instance attributes* (cf. Figure 5) are used for this purpose. In order to enable an Instantiation of instance attributes, they are labeled with an attribute of the type *marker "abstract element"* (cf. Figure 21). Thus it is possible to notify the user of the necessary concretion of the particular attribute. The *instance attribute* should not be associated with a certain *domain* in the course of model construction if the domain of the attribute is as well intended to be defined by the user. This is possible, because the cardinality of the instance attribute regarding the domain is declared as (0,1). An instance attribute therefore does not have to obtain a domain. In order to avoid that a domain allocation is forgotten for instance attributes that are not intended to be instantiated, a restriction for the relationship type *attribute has domain* is introduced, which constrains this option to instance attributes that are marked as abstract.

| ID | Type | InstAttr_ID | Attribute Name | Domain | Value |
|----|------|-------------|----------------|--------|-------|
| 123 | Function | A123 | Name | Text | Perform second check |
| 123 | Function | B123 | Average Cost | NULL | NULL |
| 777 | Event | X777 | Name | Text | Document correctness assured |
| 778 | Event | X778 | Name | Text | Second check failed |
| 628 | Job | V628 | Name | Text | Authorized personnel |
| ... | ... | ... | ... | ... | ... |

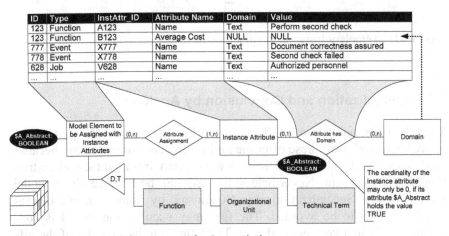

**Figure 21:** Meta model constructs for Instantiation

In addition to the running example shown in Figure 17, Figure 22 presents the exemplary Instantiation of elements and attributes of a process on

model layer. A process model – again for the "second set of eyes" principle of an initially unknown issue – is designated with appropriate attributes. These are labeled with the prefix $A for the attribute type marker
"abstract element", $ID for instance attributes with a definite domain and
$IF for instance attributes with an idle domain. The namings of all model
elements are initially formulated generally and, in the course of Instantiation, are adjusted to fit the concrete issue. The instance attribute
*$IF_average cost* of the process function is instantiated regarding both its
domain and its value as a *time* attribute with the value *15 min*. The process
function has already been refined into a process component by the reference model constructor (designated by the bold black dot annotated to the
function) but has been left idle and labeled with the attribute
*$A_abstract=TRUE*. In the course of Instantiation it is concretized trough
a process model. The example also shows that certain attributes like e. g.
the distinct identifier should not be instantiated. They therefore belong to
the conventional attribute type. The values of the instance attributes as
they turn out before Instantiation can be found in the table in Figure 21.

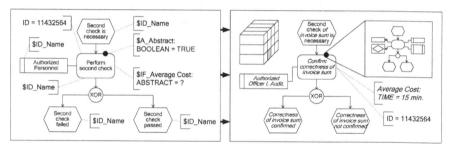

**Figure 22:** Exemplary Instantiation of a process model

## 5.4  Specialization and Conclusion by Analogy

Regarding Specialization and Conclusion by Analogy on the part of the
reference model user, these offer the highest freedom of creativity, because
guidelines about model modification are – apart from syntactical restrictions – nearly absent. Nevertheless, the user can be notified about model
sections whose Specialization resp. Conclusion by Analogy might be reasonable or has to be avoided. The first may occur if the model is consciously built in a very general way. The latter is to be expected if the reference model constructor building the model identifies the reusability of
the currently constructed model section regarding its structure or content
for another application context. Those particular model sections that are

labeled as candidates for Specialization or Conclusion by Analogy are to be specified as model element types on meta model layer resp. as instances of the entity type element type on meta-meta model layer (cf. Figure 23).

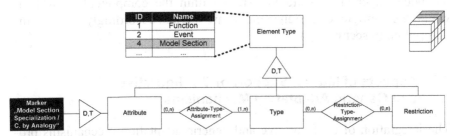

**Figure 23:** Meta-meta model constructs for Specialization and Conclusion by Analogy

The designation of a model section for the purpose of Specialization or Conclusion by Analogy is realized using attributes which belong to the type *marker "model section specialization / conclusion by analogy"*. Thus it is ensured that model sections can be reused for other purposes if they are not labeled as specializable or applicable for Conclusion by Analogy.

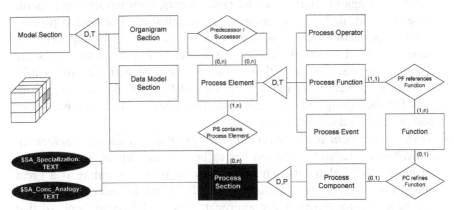

**Figure 24:** Exemplary instances of constructs supporting Specialization and Conclusion by Analogy in the process meta model

*Model sections* are specified for models of all modeling views. To avoid an additional separate meta model construct, *model sections* are specialized into *model components* and thus reused (cf. exemplary and representatively for other modeling views the specialization of *process section* into *process component* in Figure 24). The attributes marking the model sections are specified as long text fields that enable the reference model constructor to provide the model user with detailed information about possibilities of Specialization and Conclusion by Analogy in textual form.

In Figure 17, the effects of Specialization and Conclusion by Analogy on model layer are illustrated. Areas within the component as well as within the configured reference model are marked accordingly (cf. also the description in section 5.1).

## 5.5   Aspects of Mutual Support of Configurative and Generic Adaptation Mechanisms

The integration of configurative and generic adaptation mechanisms provides not only an efficient application of different adaptation strategies within a model adaptation process. The different adaptation mechanisms are rather able to support each other in order to facilitate their application through the user. In the following, we briefly outline some scenarios in which generic mechanisms support configurative mechanisms and vice versa:

- *Attribute-based Element Selection supports Aggregation*: In order to perform an aggregation of model components, appropriate components have to be located e. g. in component repositories. The search process that is dependent on characteristics of a component can be supported by Attribute-based Element Selection. Characteristics of components are stored in special attributes that belong to the type Attribute for Attribute-based Element Selection. The values of these attributes serve as inputs for the configuration mechanism that restricts the available set of components to the appropriate ones.
- *Model component declaration supports Term-based Element Selection*: Term-based Element Selection has to be prepared by assigning logical terms to model elements. This task may be time-consuming if a great amount of elements is to be assigned with a term. In order to accelerate this process, the elements are aggregated as model component, so that only one term assignment is necessary.
- *Representation Variation supports generic adaptation mechanisms*: In order to advice the reference model user regarding parts of the reference model to be modified with generic adaptation mechanisms, these parts are marked. Depending on the user, in may be necessary to change the markers' representations in order to intensify or to attenuate their appearance. Furthermore, these advices can be faded out, if a modification through generic adaptation mechanisms seems not to be appropriate for certain users.

This short list does not cover all possible mutual support scenarios. For a discussion of this issue in detail cf. [Delf06, pp. 188-206].

Furthermore, adaptation aspects which are consistently demanded but not specified by researchers, can be realized through combinations of configurative and generic adaptation mechanisms. E. g. the construction of configurable generic components is possible as well as the aggregation-supported construction of a reference model that is made configurable afterwards.

Finally, applying configuration mechanisms to generic adaptation mechanisms allows for restricting the adaptation support in further adaptation steps. E. g., if it is decided to provide configuration support but no generic adaptation support for a later adaptation step, this can be realized by applying configuration mechanisms on model element types that are responsible for the specification of generic adaptation mechanisms. In other words, configuring adaptation mechanisms allows for switching off generic adaptation mechanisms. This proceeding is reasonable if model users in later adaptation steps are less skilled. A conceptual discussion of this issue can also be found in [Delf06, pp. 188-206, pp. 234-238].

## 6   Conclusion and Outlook

In order to fit information models to specific requirements, configurative and generic adaptation mechanisms provide a useful means, since model users are partially released from adaptation efforts. This is predominantly possible via methodical support which enables an automation of several adaptation steps. Furthermore, through an integration of generic and configurative adaptation concepts on the basis of one single language framework, the combined application of these concepts is simplified. Therefore the reference modeler is provided with comprehensive design options how to ameliorate his reference model with appropriate adaptation support for the user.

Our contribution had to be restricted to the conceptual specification of the proposed adaptive concepts for reference modeling languages. Moreover, the presented running example had to be limited to one specific adaptation process. Nevertheless, one topic of further research will be the development of a procedural model that provides recommendations how and in which sequence to use the introduced adaptation concepts.

Furthermore, besides the aspects of mutual adaptation mechanism support already outlined, these will be extended and elaborated in detail in order to be able to formulate design recommendations for a modeling tool that allows for adaptive reference modeling efficiently. Thereby, especially the reduction respectively the control of the modeling and adaptation complexity is to be considered. As a result of the complexity of reference models with adaptation support the acceptance of the corresponding modeling techniques in practice is only attainable if appropriate modeling tools for those are provided. Therefore the framework is to be extended by a further dimension of the construction level of application systems – here of the modeling tools (cf. [Sche00]). For this purpose, the presented conceptual specification of adaptation mechanisms will be transformed into a design specification and implemented as a modeling tool component. We aim at using the ARIS Toolset as a basis since this tool is well-established and wide-spread.

Middle-term research activities will focus on standardization. Since there exists a great number of modeling tools, it is considered reasonable to transfer the specification of reference model adaptation concepts into a commonly readable format which is able to serve as input for scripting languages that are common in modeling tools. Through this, an easy dissemination of adaptation concepts is expected to be realized.

Long-term research can be forecasted considering the question if only certain adaptation forms are adequate for different application contexts. Against this background, the configuration of modeling languages concerning the adaptation mechanisms has to be taken into account. Thereby different adaptation mechanisms could be offered depending on the current modeling context (e. g. economic domains or modeling perspectives).

## References

[Allw98] Allweyer, T.: Modellbasiertes Wissensmanagement. Information Management & Consulting 13 (1998) 1, pp. 37-45.

[BADN03] Becker, J.; Algermissen, L.; Delfmann, P.; Niehaves, B.: Konstruktion konfigurierbarer Referenzmodelle für die öffentliche Verwaltung. In: Proceedings of the Informatik 2003. Innovative Informatikanwendungen. Frankfurt 2003, pp. 238-242.

[BDKK02] Becker, J.; Delfmann, P.; Knackstedt, R.; Kuropka, D.: Konfigurative Referenzmodellierung. In: Becker, J.; Knackstedt, R. (eds.): Wissensmanagement mit Referenzmodellen. Konzepte für die Anwendungssystem- und Organisationsgestaltung. Heidelberg 2002, pp. 25-144.

[BeDK04] Becker, J.; Delfmann, P.; Knackstedt, R.: Konstruktion von Referenzmodellierungssprachen. Ein Ordnungsrahmen zur Spezifikation von Adaptionsmechanismen für Informationsmodelle. Wirtschaftsinformatik 46 (2004) 4, pp. 251-264.

[BeKR03] Becker, J.; Kugeler, M.; Rosemann, M.: Process Management. A Guide for the Design of Business Processes. Berlin et al., Germany 2003.

[BJDF06] Becker, J.; Janiesch, C.; Delfmann, P.; Fuhr, W.: Perspectives on Process Documentation – A Case Study. In: Chen, C.-S.; Filipe, J.; Seruca, I.; Cordeiro, J. (eds.): Enterprise Information Systems VII. Dordrecht 2006, S. 167-177.

[BKKD01] Becker, J.; Knackstedt, R.; Kuropka, D.; Delfmann, P.: Subjektivitätsmanagement für die Referenzmodellierung: Vorgehensmodell und Werkzeugkonzept. In: Proceedings of the KnowTech 2001. Dresden 2001.

[Broc03] Vom Brocke, J.: Referenzmodellierung. Gestaltung und Verteilung von Konstruktionsprozessen. Berlin 2003.

[Chen76] Chen, P. P.-S.: The Entity-Relationship Model. Toward a Unified View of Data. ACM Transactions on Database-Systems 1 (1976) 1, pp. 9-36.

[DaSh96] Darke, P.; Shanks, G.: Stakeholder Viewpoints in Requirements Definition. Requirements Engineering, 1 (1996) 1, pp. 88-105.

[Delf06] Delfmann, P.: Adaptive Referenzmodellierung. Methodische Konzepte zur Konstruktion und Anwendung wiederverwendungsorientierter Informationsmodelle. Berlin 2006.

[FeYu00] Fernandez, E. B.; Yuan, X.: Semantic Analysis Patterns. In : Laender, A. H. F.; Liddle, S. W.; Storey, S. W. (eds.): Conceptual Modeling – ER 2000 – 19th International Conference on Conceptual Modeling, Salt Lake City 2000, pp. 183-195.

[Fran99] Frank, U.: Conceptual Modelling as the Core of the Information Systems Discipline – Perspectives and Epistemological Challenges. In: Proceedings of Americas Conference on Information Systems – AMCIS '99, Milwaukee 1999, pp. 695-698.

[HaPS99] Han, T.-D.; Purao, S.; Storey, V. C.: A Methodology for Building a Repository of Object-Oriented Design Fragments. In: Akoka, J.; M. Bouzeghoub, M; Comyn-Wattiau, I.; Métais, E. (eds.): Conceptual Modeling – ER '99 – 18th International Conference on Conceptual Modeling. Paris 1999, pp. 203-217.

[ISO96] ISO14977 (1996). Information technology – Syntactic Metalanguage – Extended BNF.

[KeNS92] Keller, G.; Nüttgens, M.; Scheer, A.-W.: Semantische Prozeßmodellierung auf der Grundlage Ereignisgesteuerter Prozeßketten (EPK). Veröffentlichungen des Instituts für Wirtschaftsinformatik, Heft 89. Saarbrücken, 1992.

[Kilo91] Kilov, H.: Generic information modeling concepts: a reusable component library. In: Bézivin, J.; Meyer, B. (eds.): Proceedings of the Fourth international Conference on Technology of Object-Oriented Languages and Systems. Upper Saddle River 1991, pp. 187-201.

[KlMy99] Klein, H. K.; Myers, M. D.: A set of principles for conducting and evaluating interpretive field studies in information systems. MIS Quarterly. 23 (1999) 1, pp. 67-93.

[NJJZ96] Nissen, H. W.; Jeusfeld, M.; Jarke, M.; Zemanek, G. V.; Huber, H.: Managing Multiple Requirements Perspectives with Metamodels. IEEE Software 13 (1996) 2, pp. 37-48.

[Risi00] Rising, L: The Pattern Almanac 2000. Boston et al., USA 2000.

[RoAa07] Rosemann, M.; van der Aalst, W. M. P.: A Configurable Reference Modelling Language. Information Systems 23 (2007) 1, S. 1-23.

[RoGr00] Rosemann, M.; Green, P.: Integrating multi-perspective views into ontological analysis. In: 21st International Conference on Information Systems. Brisbane 2000, pp. 618-627.

[Rose03] Rosemann, M.: Application Reference Models and Building Blocks for Management and Control. In: Bernus, P.; Nemes, L.; Schmidt, G.: Handbook of Enterprise Architecture. Berlin et al. 2003, pp. 595-615.

[Rose98] Rosemann, M.: Managing the Complexity of Multiperspective Information Models using the Guidelines of Modeling. In: Fowler, D.; Dawson, L. (eds.): Proceedings of the 3rd Australian Conference on Requirements Engineering. Geelong 1998, pp. 101-118.

[Sche00] Scheer, A.-W.: ARIS - Business Process Modeling. 3rd edition, Berlin et al. 2000.

[Silv01] Silverston, L.: The Data Model Resource Book, Volume 2. A Library of Data Models for Specific Industries. 2001.

[SoGD03] Soffer, P.; Golany, B.; Dori, D.: ERP modeling: a comprehensive approach. Information Systems 28 (2003) 9, pp. 673-690.

[Stra96] Strahringer, S.: Metamodellierung als Instrument des Methodenvergleichs. Eine Evaluierung am Beispiel objektorientierter Analysemethoden. Aachen, Germany 1996.

[Szyp02] Szyperski, C.: Component Software – Beyond Object-Oriented Programming. 2nd edition, London et al. 2002.

[Weic95] Weick, K. E.: Sensemaking in Organizations. Thousand Oaks, CA, USA, 1995.

[WMBK03] Wigand, R.T.; Mertens, P.; Bodendorf, F.; König, W.; Picot, A.; Schumann, M.: Introduction to Business Information Systems. Berlin et al., Germany 2003.

# Configurable Process Models – A Foundational Approach

Florian Gottschalk, Wil M. P. van der Aalst, Monique H. Jansen-Vullers

*Abstract: Off-the-shelf packages such as SAP need to be configured to suit the requirements of an organization. Reference models support the configuration of these systems. Existing reference models use rather traditional languages. For example, the SAP reference model uses Event-driven Process Chains (EPCs). Unfortunately, the choice construct within traditional process modeling languages like EPCs do not capture different scopes or impacts of decisions. That means they offer no opportunities to distinguish between decisions made for a single case (i. e. process instance) when executing the process and decisions made in advance for numerous cases impacting bigger parts of the company. This paper discusses the need for configurable process models. An analysis of configuration from a theoretical perspective provides a solid fundament for such models. Within the analysis a link is made to inheritance of dynamic behavior and previously defined inheritance concepts. By applying these concepts to process models the essence of configuration is determined, which enables the development of more mature configurable process modeling languages.*

## 1    Introduction

Reference models streamline the design of particular models by providing a generic solution [RoAa05]. Motivated by the "Design by Reuse" paradigm they provide a repository of potentially relevant models which can be used to accelerate the modeling process. Ideally these models are "plug and play" but usually need some adjustment to individual requirements [Bern99; FeLo02; BeDK04; ADGR06]. Hereby it is required to distinguish between *generating* and *non-generating* adaptations. Non-generating adaptations as Aggregation, Instantiation, Specialization, and Analogy are providing basic models with certain gaps which have to be filled in by the reference model user. That means, the individual part of the model is generated by the user and not by guidelines of the reference model. The reference model only provides interfaces. A generating approach on the other hand provides clear rules how the reference model can be configured and therefore adapted to the user's requirements [BeDK04; Schü98; Schw99; BrBu04]. Unfortunately, the languages used for reference modeling provide little or no support to include such different configuration options [BeKR03; CuKe97; Rose03]. The goal of this paper is to discuss the theoretical requirements for *configurable process modeling languages*, i. e., we restrict ourselves to the control-flow perspective [JaBu96].

Probably the most comprehensive reference model is the SAP reference model [CuKe97]. Its data model includes more than 4000 entity types and the reference process models cover more than 1000 business processes and inter-organizational business scenarios [RoAa05]. Most of the other dominant ERP vendors have similar or alternative approaches towards reference models. Foundational conceptual work for the SAP reference model has been conducted by SAP AG and the Institute for Information Systems (IWi) of the Saarland University in a collaborative research project in the years 1990-1992 [KeNS92]. The outcome of this project was the process modeling language Event-Driven Process Chains (EPCs) [KeNS92; Kind04], which has been used for the design of the reference process models in SAP. EPCs also became the core modeling language in the Architecture of Integrated Information Systems (ARIS) [Sche94; Sche00]. It is now one of the most popular reference modeling languages and has also been used for the design of many SAP-independent reference models (e. g., the ARIS-based reference model for Siebel CRM or industry models for banking, retail, insurance, telecommunication, etc.). *Despite its success, the basic EPC model offers little support for process configuration.* It contains (X)OR connectors but it is unclear whether the corresponding decisions need to be taken at run-time (e. g., based on the stock-level), at build-time (e. g., based on the size of the organization using SAP), or somewhere in-between (e. g., based on the period of the year or resource availability). For that reason so-called *Configurable EPCs* (C-EPCs) were developed [RoAa05; DRAS05], extending EPCs (and previously developed extensions like build-time operators [Schü98; RoSc97; Rose96]), aiming at a generic-monolithic approach for constructing re-usable models [FeLo02]. Indeed C-EPCs allow for a clear distinction between run-time and build-time decisions. However, they only provide a partial solution as they are based on a specific language (i. e. EPCs). Within this paper we will look at configuration from an language-independent perspective. Afterwards we will use the results to analyze C-EPCs [RoAa05].

The remainder of the paper is organized as follows. First, we elaborate on the concept of "choice" which is essential for configurable process models. Second, we approach the problem from a theoretical viewpoint, i. e., we depict what the essence of configuration is. Finally, we briefly discuss Configurable EPCs as a first step towards such configurable process models.

## 2  It Is All About Making Choices

There are many languages to model processes ranging from formal (e. g., Petri nets and process algebras such as Pi calculus) to informal (flow charts, UML activity diagrams, EPCs, etc.). Each of these languages provides some *notion of choice* (e. g., two transitions sharing a single input place in a Petri net, the "+"-operator in process algebra, the $\Diamond$-symbol in UML activity diagrams, or an (X)OR-split connector in an EPC). Typically, it is not possible to describe the nature of such a choice. At best one can either specify a Boolean condition based on some data element (data-based decision) or one can specify events that have to occur for triggering paths (event-based decision) [OwRa03]. The usual interpretation is that a choice is made at run-time, based on such a Boolean condition or based on occurring events. *In the context of reference models, this interpretation is too narrow.*

The *scope* of a decision can vary. For example, if a hospital uses a rule like "If a patient has high blood pressure a day before the planned operation, the operation will be cancelled", then the scope of each choice (operate or not) is limited to a single patient. There may also be choices which affect more cases, e. g., consider the rule "If there is a major disaster in the region, all planned operations will be cancelled." or also an entire process, e. g., "The admittance process requires patients to pre-register". There may even be choices that affect all processes within an organization. We call such choices that are made in advance and that are affecting more than a single instance of a process *configuration choices*. However note that the borderline between run-time choices and configuration choices may be a bit fuzzy as the following examples show.

- The organization's management chooses not to allow for pre-shipments.
- The Dutch branches require a deposit, while this is not needed for branches in other countries (nation-wide management decision).
- If stock is below 100 items, only preferred customers are serviced (local management decision).
- Based on the volume of the order, the goods are shipped by truck or mail (local management decision).
- On Saturday, goods are shipped by truck (local, temporal decision).

Each of these choices is at another level, i. e. they are made at other points in time with different validity limits and periods. However, classical process modeling languages, e. g., the languages used in workflow management systems [AaHe02; JaBu96] or in reference modeling [CuKe97], allow only for one level of choice. The examples demonstrate that reference models have to allow for a broader spectrum of choices. All decisions have in common that they restrict the actual available options for decisions at a later point in time. For that reason one can view configuration as *limiting choices by making choices*. However, at a certain point in time it is not longer possible to postpone a decision without delaying the actual process flow. These decisions are called run-time decision and must be distinguished from build-time or configuration decisions which can be postponed to a later point in time without delaying the process flow. Seen from this viewpoint, process modeling languages need to distinguish at least between run-time choices and configuration choices.

## 3    Configuration: A Theoretical Perspective

The aim of configurable process models is to provide generic models integrating possible process variations into one model. Afterwards such a model can be configured to a specific solution. This means a configurable model should guide the user to a solution that fits to the user's requirements [BeDK04]. In [FeLo02] this is also classified as a generic-monolithic approach for model re-use. In order to provide such configuration opportunities *a configurable model must be able to provide a complete, integrated set of all possible process configurations*. Only in this case each individual model can be derived from the model. In other words the configurable process model can be described as the "least common multiple" of all process variations. The task of configuration is to create a new model by selecting that parts of the configurable model that are relevant to the user or – the other way around – by deselecting the irrelevant parts. In practice such a configured process model can probably not satisfy all individual requirements as the reference model will not include the complete set of all possible configurations. The gap has to be filled in manually by the user by applying non-generating adaptation mechanisms [BeDK04]. However this subsequent step is out of the scope of this paper.

   To depict and analyze process models we will use the notion of *Labeled Transition Systems (LTS)*.

**Definition 1:** *A labeled transition system is a five-tuple LTS = (S, L, T, $S_I$, $S_F$), where*

- S is the set of states,
- L is the set of transition labels,
- $\tau \in L$ is the label reserved for silent transitions,
- $T \subseteq S \times L \times S$ is the set of transitions,

- $S_I \subseteq S$ is the set of initial states, and
- $S_F \subseteq S$ is the set of final states.

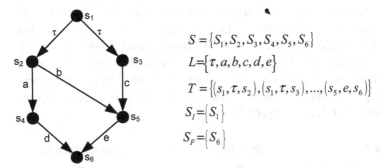

$$S = \{S_1, S_2, S_3, S_4, S_5, S_6\}$$

$$L = \{\tau, a, b, c, d, e\}$$

$$T = \{(s_1, \tau, s_2), (s_1, \tau, s_3), ..., (s_5, e, s_6)\}$$

$$S_I = \{S_1\}$$

$$S_F = \{S_6\}$$

**Figure 1:** A labeled transition system

A state represents a complete set of properties, describing the actual situation within the process. A labeled transition describes the switching from one state to another. Therefore transitions are also representing any kind of activity or functionality that is executed and thereby changing the properties of the system. LTS can be depicted graphically as, e. g., in Figure 1. The actual process flow is from top to bottom. E. g., the execution of the transition labeled "a" transforms $S_2$ into $S_4$. If more than one outgoing arc leaves a state, there is a choice between the arcs for the continuation of the process. A silent transition, labeled $\tau$, is a special transition that transforms a state into another without changing any of the externally visible properties of the state. Note that in $S_1$ all three transitions $a$, $b$, and $c$ can be executed, in $S_2$ only $a$ and $b$ can be executed, and in $S_3$ only $c$ can be executed, i. e., although the $\tau$ transitions are not visible they may limit the possible ways to continue.

Although numerous process modeling languages are defined and used, all process models having formal semantics can be mapped onto labeled transition systems [BaAa01; GlWe96; Miln80]. By using labeled transition systems for our analysis, we are able to transfer the results into any of these languages.

To depict the essence of configuration we make use of the concepts of *inheritance of dynamic behavior* [AaBb02; BaAa01]. The basic idea of inheritance – as also applied in object-oriented software development – is to provide a mechanism that allows constructing subclasses which are inheriting all behavior and features of superclasses. The subclass extends the superclass with additional behavior or features, i. e., the superclass supports less functionality than the subclass. By using multiple inheritance it is also possible that a subclass is the subclass of multiple superclasses.

Such a subclass includes the behavior of all superclasses, i. e. from the perspective of each single superclass the subclass is extended with the behavior of the other superclasses. If such a subclass is minimal (i. e., each extension is motivated by some superclass), we refer to it as the least common multiple of all superclasses. In this paper, we will show that this least common multiple corresponds to the unconfigured reference model. Each superclass of the subclass (i. e., the reference model) can be regarded as one of its configured variants. That means configuration is the process of transforming the subclass into the superclass, which is exactly the inverse of inheritance (cf. also Figure 2).

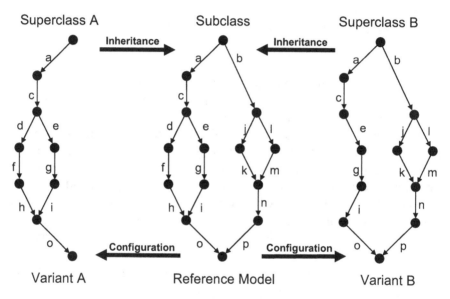

**Figure 2:** Configuration – the inverse of inheritance

In [AaBa02; BaAa01] two different mechanisms for detecting inheritance in workflow models are defined. Both mechanisms are defined in the inverse direction. That means the behavior of the superclass is regarded from the viewpoint of the subclass. The first mechanism inhibits the execution of additionally functionality. If it is not possible to distinguish the behaviors of model $x$ and model $y$ when only transitions of $x$ that are also present in $y$ are executed, then $x$ will be a subclass of $y$. That means all transitions of the subclass $x$ that are not present in the superclass $y$ are *blocked* (encapsulation). The second mechanism compares the effects of the superclass $y$ and subclass $x$ by considering only that effects of the subclass $x$ that also occur within the superclass $y$. If it is not possible to distinguish the behaviors of $x$ and $y$ when arbitrary tasks of $x$ are executed, but when only the effects of tasks that are also present in $y$ are considered, then $x$ is a subclass of $y$. All effects of the subclass $x$ not occurring in $y$ are *hidden* in the superclass $y$ (abstraction).

When configuring a process model, the complete, configurable model is restricted to a desired variant. As the two mechanisms of blocking and hiding are defined in the inverse direction and as we showed that configuration can be regarded as the inverse of inheritance we can use these mechanisms to depict configuration in the following. However, as shown above, configuration implies decision making. Each configuration decision of blocking/not blocking or hiding/not hiding determines if a transition will be executable at run-time or not. A decision, however, requires information which might not be available at build-time. Such decisions must be postponed to run-time and performed for each case individually. Therefore they must be integrated into a run-time (i. e., configured) process model. Thus, a transition can not only be configured as hidden or blocked but also as optional hidden or optional blocked. That means for an LTS:

**Definition 2:** *A configuration is a (partial) function* $c \in T \nrightarrow \{\tau, \delta, \tau_0, \delta_0\}$ *where dom (c) is the set of configured transitions, and for* $t \in dom(c)$ *(* $f \in A \nrightarrow B$ *denotes a partial function,* $dom(f) \subseteq A$ *is the domain of* $f$ *):*

- $c(t) = \tau$, is a hidden transition,
- $c(t) = \delta$, is a blocked transition,
- $c(t) = \tau_0$, is a optionally hidden transition, and
- $c(t) = \delta_0$, is a optionally blocked transition.

Of course not all configurations are possible and therefore valid. E. g., for sure certain functionality and therefore certain transitions are mandatory and cannot be blocked or hidden. Also interdependencies between various transitions will probably exist. Therefore we define:

**Definition 3:** *A configurable process model is a tuple CPM = (LTS, CS) where:*

- $LTS = (S, L, T, S_I, S_F)$ is a labeled transition system, and
- $CS \subseteq T \nrightarrow \{\tau, \delta, \tau_0, \delta_0\}$ is a set of configurations.

Configuring the configurable process model means to select a configuration $c \in CS$. To get a configured model the configuration must be applied to the labeled transition system. Figure 3 depicts some configuration-examples within an LTS. The first column depicts the configurable models. The subsequent columns depict the configured models of certain configuration scenarios.

The configuration decision to *block* a transition implies that the transition will never be executed. That means the transition should not appear within the configured model. It must be removed from the model when transforming the configurable model into a configured model as depicted in Figure 3a/b. The configurable transition $a$ in Figure 3a is removed in the configured model in Figure 3b. As no alternative transition can be executed from state $S_1$ the state becomes a deadlock. State $S_2$ and subsequent transitions and states become unreachable. They could be removed from the configured model, however as they are not reachable anyway this has no influence on the execution of the process. This situation differs from the situation if transition $a$ is configured blocked in the second configurable model (Figure 3d). In this case transition $b$ must be executed when reaching $S_1$ (Figure 3e).

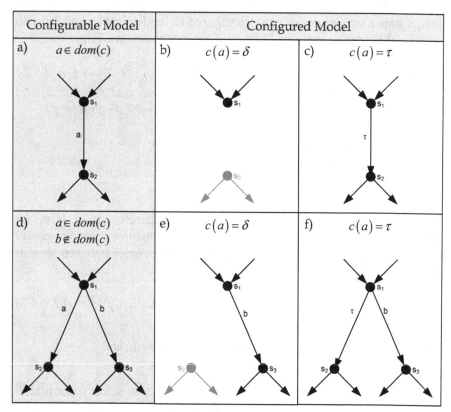

**Figure 3:** Configuration in a labeled transition system

If the configuration decision is to *hide* a transition, the transition's external, i. e. observable, effects will be ignored. However the effects within the model, that means on the execution of subsequent transitions, are kept. Therefore, when transforming the configurable model into a configured model, the transition must be transformed into a silent step without output by renaming the label into $\tau$ (cf. Figure 3a/c). The definition of hiding given above explicitly says that the task is executed, but the external effect is ignored. However, the desired result when configuring a process model differs slightly. In fact instead of ignoring the transition's external effects it should not even be executed. Only the non-observable, internal effect of reaching a subsequent state and triggering subsequent transitions has to occur. For that reason we will call this kind of configuration also *skipping* in the following. As the perceived results are identical, skipping can be handled in the same manner as hiding by introducing a silent step $\tau$.

If it is not possible to decide on hiding/blocking at configuration time, a configured model can – as depicted above – include the choice between blocking and not blocking or between hiding and not hiding. To include such a postponed choice into the configured model, the choice must of course be included before the actual transition. Each postponed configuration decision needs to be resolved at run-time; either the transition will be hidden/blocked or it will not be hidden/not be blocked. In order to model such as run-time decision, we introduce new intermediate states into the model. Each state corresponds to the result of all postponed decisions in the particular state. We denote these as states $s_{H,NH,B,NB}$ where $H \subseteq T$ is the set of hidden transitions in the particular state, $NH \subseteq T$ are the non-hidden transitions, $B \subseteq T$ are the blocked transitions, and $NB \subseteq T$ are the non-blocked transitions. If it is obvious which transition is referred to, we just use the label to describe a labeled transition, i. e. we write $l$ instead of $(s, l, s')$. E. g., in Figure 4b the transition labeled $a$ is configured as optional blocked. For that reason two additional states are introduced within the configured model: $s_{1\{\},\{\},\{\},\{a\}}$ for the case that $a$ will not be blocked at run-time and $s_{1\{\},\{\},\{a\},\{\}}$ for the case that $a$ will be blocked at run-time. For the subsequent model each state matches exactly $s_1$ of the case that it would have been configured blocked or not blocked at build-time, i. e. for example $s_{1\{\},\{\},\{a\},\{\}}$ matches $s_1$ in Figure 3b. It represents the deadlock. Both states $s_{1\{\},\{\},\{a\},\{\}}$ and $s_{1\{\},\{\},\{\},\{a\}}$ are reachable from $s_1$ by silent transitions. As these silent transitions have no output, the execution of the model will result in the same process as if the configuration decision would have been made at build-time.

Figure 4c depicts the same situation for the case that transition $a$ is configured as optionally hidden. Here state $s_{1\{\},\{a\},\{\},\{\}}$ represents the situation that transition $a$ is not hidden and will be executed, whereas $s_{1\{a\},\{\},\{\},\{\}}$ represents the result of the configuration decision to hide transition $a$ and therefore corresponds to $s_1$ in Figure 3c. Figures 4e/f provide further examples by depicting the optional configurations of $a$ in figures 3e/f.

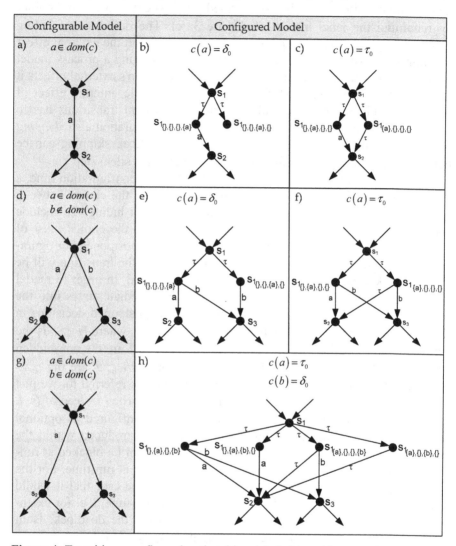

**Figure 4:** Transitions configured optional in a labeled transition system

Figure 4h depicts a situation where more than one transition that is outgoing from the same state is configured optional. In this case it is required to generate $2^n$ intermediate states, where n is the number of transitions that are configured optional. The sets *H*, *NH*, *B*, and *NB* depict the configurations of the transition. They define which configuration is represented by the particular state.

To transform the configurable process model into a configured process model we provide the following algorithm:

**Algorithm 1.** *Let* LTS $= (S, L, T, S_I, S_F)$ *be a labeled transition system and* $c \in T \nrightarrow \{\tau, \delta, \tau_0, \delta_0\}$ *a configuration. The labeled transition system resulting from this configuration, notation* $LTS^c = (S^c, L^c, T^c, S_I^c, S_F^c)$, *is defined as follows:*

- $T_0 = \{t \in dom(c) \mid c(t) \in \{\tau_0, \delta_0\}\}$,

- $S_0 = \{s \in S \mid \exists_{(s',l,s'') \in T_0} s' = s\}$,

- $T' = \{t \in T \mid t \in dom(c) \Rightarrow c(t) \in \{\tau_0, \delta_0\}\} \cup$
  $\{(s, \tau, s') \mid \exists_{l \in L} (s, l, s') \in dom(c) \wedge c((s, l, s')) = \tau\}$,

- $S_{opt} = \{s_{H,NH,B,NB} \mid s \in S_0$
  $\wedge (H \cap NH = \varnothing)$
  $\wedge \left(H \cup NH = \{(s', l, s'') \in T_0 \mid s = s' \wedge c((s', l, s'')) = \tau_0\}\right)$
  $\wedge (B \cap NB = \varnothing)$
  $\wedge \left(B \cup NB = \{(s', l, s'') \in T_0 \mid s = s' \wedge c((s', l, s'')) = \delta_0\}\right)$
  $\}$,

- $T_{opt} = \{(s, \tau, s_{H,NH,B,NB}) \mid s_{H,NH,B,NB} \in S_{opt}\} \cup$
  $\{(s_{H,NH,B,NB}, l, s') \mid s_{H,NH,B,NB} \in S_{opt} \wedge l \in (NH \cup NB) \wedge (s, l, s') \in T'\} \cup$
  $\{(s_{H,NH,B,NB}, \tau, s') \mid s_{H,NH,B,NB} \in S_{opt} \wedge \exists l \in H : (s, l, s') \in T'\} \cup$
  $\{(s_{H,NH,B,NB}, l, s') \mid s_{H,NH,B,NB} \in S_{opt} \wedge (s, l, s') \in (T' \setminus T_0) \wedge s \in S_0\}$,

- $S^c = S \cup S_{opt}$,

- $L^c = L$,

- $T^c = \{(s', l, s'') \in T' \mid s' \notin S_0\} \cup T_{opt}$,

- $S_I^c = S_I$, and

- $S_F^c = S_F$.

$T_0$ is the set of transitions configured as either optionally hidden or optionally blocked. $S_0$ are all states which are sources of transitions configured as optional. $T'$ are all transitions of the configurable model that are not configured as blocked or hidden, merged with the transitions that are configured as hidden with changed labels to $\tau$. $S_{opt}$ are all the additional intermediate states required for including postponed configuration choices. $T_{opt}$ are all transitions required to include $S_{opt}$ into the model. There are four types of transitions. First, $T_{opt}$ includes all the silent transitions from the original states to the intermediate states. Second, it includes the original transitions repositioned between all new intermediate states in which they are listed in "NB" or in "NH" and their original targets. Third, $T_{opt}$ includes all the renamed, silent transitions from the intermediate states where they are listed in "H" to their original target. Fourth, it also includes all non-configured transitions originally leaving a state in $S_0$, reallocated between the particular intermediate state and its original destination. Of course, blocked transitions must not be included here.

These sets enable us to specify the configured model. Labels, initial states, and final states remain the same as in the configurable model. The states of the configured model $S^c$ are the states of the unconfigured model $S$ plus the states required for the postponed choices $S_{opt}$. To define the transitions of the configured model, $T^c$ consists of two types of transitions. First, $T^c$ includes all the non-configured or hidden transitions defined in $T'$, but without the transitions leaving a state that is split into intermediate states. Second, the transitions to include the intermediate states into the model are defined in $T_{opt}$ and also included in $T^c$.

Some states and transitions become unreachable within such a configured labeled transition system. An additional cleanup algorithm could of course remove these elements. Since this is a trivial technicality it is not shown here.

After clearly defining what configuration of process models is and after defining what configurable process models formally are, we are now able to systematically analyze existing configurable process modeling languages and propose improvements.


# 4    Configurable EPCs: An Example of a Language

To conclude this paper we will introduce and analyze *Configurable EPCs* (C-EPCs) [RoAa05; DRAS05]. C-EPCs serve as an example of a configurable process modeling language and we compare its expressive power with the requirements for process configuration. C-EPCs are an extension of EPCs [KeNS92]. An EPC consists of functions, events, arcs, and connectors. Events represent states and functions represent activities or functionality. Arcs and connectors define the process flow. Functions follow events and events follow functions. Moreover, to model splits and joins in a process, connectors may be used. There are three types of connectors: AND, OR and XOR.

AND-splits and AND-joins may be used to model parallel routing. XOR-splits and XOR-joins may be used to model the selection of specific routes (e. g., a "switch case" construct). OR-splits and OR-joins may be used to model a mixture of conditional and parallel routing. (The depicted semantics are informal. There is an on-going discussion about mathematical sound semantics of EPCs, especially on the non-locality of the OR-join, e. g. cf. [Kind06; AaDK02].)

In a C-EPC, as defined in [RoAa05; DRAS05], *both functions and connectors may be configurable.* Configurable functions may be included (ON), skipped (OFF) or conditionally skipped (OPT). Configurable connectors may be restricted at build-time, e. g., a configurable connector of type OR may be mapped onto an AND connector, an XOR-connector or a sequence (for details cf. [RoAa05], Section 5.2). Local configuration choices like skipping a function may be limited by configuration requirements. For example, if one configurable function $f_1$ is configured as "ON", then another configurable function $f_2$ needs to be excluded. This configuration requirement may be denoted by the logical expression $f_1 = ON \Rightarrow f_2 = OFF$. In addition to these requirements it is possible to add guidelines, supporting the configuration process.

Figure 5 shows a C-EPC describing an invoice verification process. The classical EPC is extended with configurable functions and connectors (indicated using thick lines) as well as with requirements and guidelines attached to functions. For example function *Invoicing Plan Settlement* (i) is configurable, i. e., it may be included (ON), skipped (OFF) or conditionally skipped (OPT) within the configured model. Note that skipping corresponds to the notion of hiding, i. e., if a function is skipped, the process flow continues after the function without actually executing the function. This is also depicted in the first row of Figure 6. The function $a$ within the C-EPC process fragment is switched "OFF". This conforms to a hidden transition $a$ within the corresponding LTS. Within the configured LTS, the transition is renamed into $\tau$, whereas in the configured EPC function $a$ is removed. In order to generate a lawful EPC also one of the events surrounding $a$ must be removed, which is indicated by the brackets around event $A$ in Figure 6. Comparing the configured EPC and the configured LTS, the sequences of executed activities correspond to each other. Also optional hiding is supported by C-EPCs: If a function is configured as "OPT" this means that the decision about its execution is postponed to run-time [MRRA05; DRAS05].

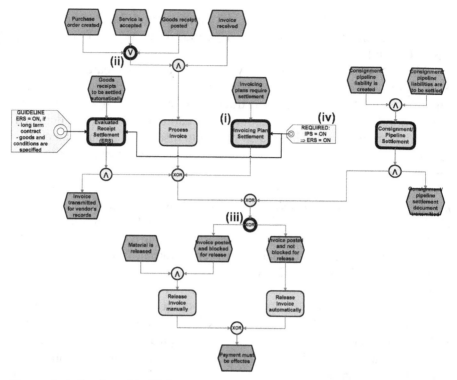

**Figure 5:** A Configurable EPC

The example C-EPC in Figure 5 also shows two configurable connectors. By configuring the OR-join (ii), it is possible to specify which of the events has to occur in order to start the process. E. g., it is possible to restrict the connector to an AND-join, which would mean that all events have to occur. It is also possible to restrict it to an XOR-join which would mean that only one of the events has to occur. The configurable XOR-split (iii) can be configured to an XOR-connector or it can be restricted to a sequence. E. g., to disable automatic invoice release, it can be configured to a sequence only executing the left path (i. e. always performing manual invoice release). In fact this conforms to blocking of the other path leaving the XOR connector. The second row of Figure 6 depicts a process fragment of a corresponding labeled transition system. In the third row of this Figure it becomes obvious that direct blocking of functionality is not available within C-EPCs. There is no construct available that would enable the blocking of function *b* as it is in the labeled transition system. A configurable function can only be hidden, but not blocked. That means within C-EPCs blocking is only supported indirectly by configurable connectors. This also becomes obvious if it is required to postpone the choice of blocking to run-time. A configurable connector cannot be configured as optional. However if it is not restricted, it keeps all configuration opportunities. That means, the configuration choice will occur implicitly within the configured model, however it will not be modeled explicitly.

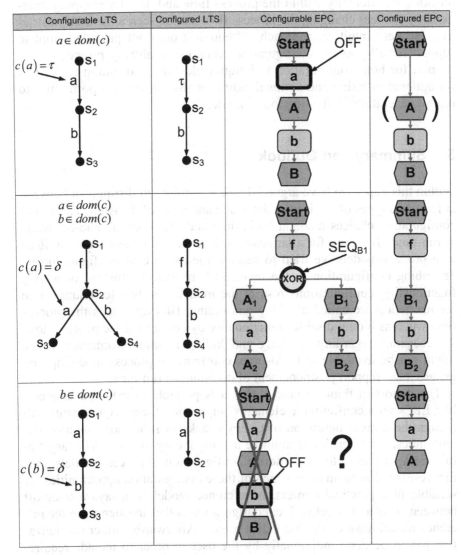

**Figure 6:** Configuration within LTSs and C-EPCs

The third element type for configuration within C-EPCs are requirements. E. g., in Figure 5 the requirement attached to "Invoicing Plan Settlement" states that if it is switched "ON" also the function *Evaluated Receipt Set-*

*tlement* has to be switched "ON" (iv). Requirements therefore ensure that only configurations are generated that are valid within the configurable process model (cf. Definition 3).

Altogether the implementation of configuration within C-EPCs by blocking functionality within the process flow and directly skipping functionality without changing the process flow can be seen as a rather restrictive, but very intuitive, approach. Although it does not provide complete support for all possible configuration scenarios, it already provides some support for both configuration techniques blocking and hiding as well as for optional blocking and optional hiding. It also provides opportunities to inhibit generation of invalid process models.

## 5   Summary and Outlook

Within this paper we have argued that it is required to distinguish between at least two types of choices as the scope and level of decisions varies: (1) configuration choices made at build-time and (2) "normal" choices made at run-time. To allow for a language-independent discussion on configurable process-models we tried to capture the essence of configuration by describing configuration as the inverse of inheritance. Instead of adding functionality, configurations restrict the model. The two techniques used for restriction are called blocking and hiding. Blocking stops the process flow whereas hiding disables functionality by continuing the process flow. As decisions regarding blocking and hiding require information which might not be available at build-time, configurable process modeling languages must support postponement of decisions to run-time.

The important thing to note is that it is possible to extend a language like EPCs with configurable elements, supporting these requirements. Although the current definition of C-EPCs lacks of some configuration opportunities, the extension is intuitive making it easy to apply. The target of this research was to formally define configuration of process models. Further research has to analyze which of these configuration opportunities are sensible in a practical context. A reference model is always a trade-off between costs and benefits. I. e. configuration is the first step from the reference model towards the individual model. Afterwards further specialization has to be done individually by the user in order to include requirements not covered by the reference model.

Using the theory developed within this paper on the one hand and practical experiences using C-EPCs on the other hand, we hope to develop more mature configuration languages. To improve the configuration process of Enterprise systems it will also be required to transfer the presented ideas from process modeling to truly executable models which can be used for enactment. As a starting point, we plan to work on adding configurability features to workflow modeling languages like *SAP workflow*, *Staffware*, or *YAWL* [RDBS02; Staf00; AaHo05].

# References

[AaBa02] van der Aalst, W. M. P.; Basten, T: Inheritance of workflows: an approach to tackling problems related to change. Theoretical Computer Science 270 (2002) 1-2, pp. 125-203.

[AaDK02] van der Aalst, W. M. P.; Desel, J.; Kindler, E.: On the Semantics of EPCs: A Vicious Circle. In: Nüttgens, M.; Rump, F. J. (eds.): Proceedings of the EPK 2002: Business Process Management using EPCs. Bonn 2002, pp. 71-80.

[AaHe02] van der Aalst, W. M. P.; van Hee, K. M.: Workflow Management: Models, Methods, and Systems. Cambridge 2002.

[AaHo05] van der Aalst W. M. P.; ter Hofstede, A. H. M.: YAWL: Yet Another Workflow Language. Information Systems 30 (2005) 4, pp. 245-275.

[ADGR06] van der Aalst, W. M. P.; Dreiling, A.; Gottschalk, F.; Rosemann, M.; Jansen-Vullers, M. H.: Configurable Process Models as a Basis for Reference Modeling. In: Bussler, C.; Haller, A. (eds.): Business Process Management Workshops: BPM 2005 International Workshops, BPI, BPD, ENEI, BPRM, WSCOBPM, BPS. Revised Selected Papers. Volume 3812 of Lecture Notes in Computer Science. Berlin et al. 2006, pp. 512-518.

[BaAa01] Basten, T.; van der Aalst, W. M. P.: Inheritance of behavior. Journal of Logic and Algebraic Programming 47 (2001) 2, pp. 47-145.

[BeDK04] Becker, J.; Delfmann, P.; Knackstedt, R.: Konstruktion von Referenzmodellierungssprachen: Ein Ordnungsrahmen zur Spezifikation von Adaptionsmechanismen für Informationsmodelle. Wirtschaftsinformatik 46 (2004) 4, pp. 251-264.

[BeKR03] Becker, J.; Kugeler, M.; Rosemann, M. (eds.): Process Management: A Guide for the Design of Business Processes. Berlin et al. 2003.

[Bern99] Bernus, P.: Generalised Enterprise Reference Architecture and Methodology, Version 1.6.3. IFIP–IFAC Task Force on Architectures for Enterprise Integration, March 1999.

[BrBu04] vom Brocke, J.; Buddendick, C.: Konstruktionstechniken für die Referenzmodellierung In: Becker, J.; Delfmann, P. (eds.): Referenzmodellierung. Grundlagen, Techniken und domänenbezogene Anwendung. Heidelberg 2004, pp. 19-48.

[CuKe97] Curran, T.; Keller, G.: SAP R/3 Business Blueprint: Understanding the Business Process Reference Model. Upper Saddle River 1997.

[DRAS05] Dreiling, A.; Rosemann, M.; van der Aalst, W. M. P.; Sadiq, W.; Khan, S.: Model-Driven Process Configuration of Enterprise Systems. In: Ferstl, O. K.; Sinz, E. J.; Eckert, S.; Isselhorst, T. (eds.): Wirtschaftsinformatik 2005. eEconomy, eGovernment, eSociety. Heidelberg 2005, pp. 687-706.

[FeLo02] Fettke, P.; Loos, P.: Methoden zur Wiederverwendung von Referenzmodellen – Übersicht und Taxonomie. In: Becker, J.; Knackstedt, R. (eds.): Referenzmodellierung 2002: Methoden – Modelle – Erfahrungen. Münster 2002, pp. 9-33.

[GlWe96] van Glabbeek, R. J.; Weijland, W. P.: Branching Time and Abstraction in Bisimulation Semantics. Journal of the ACM 43 (1996) 3, pp. 555-600.

[JaBu96] Jablonski, S.; Bussler, C.: Workflow Management: Modeling Concepts, Architecture, and Implementation. London 1996.

[KeNS92] Keller, G.; Nüttgens, M.; Scheer, A.-W.: Semantische Prozeßmodellierung auf der Grundlage Ereignisgesteuerter Prozeßketten (EPK). Veröffentlichungen des Instituts für Wirtschaftsinformatik, Heft 89. Saarbrücken, 1992.

[Kind04] Kindler, E.: On the Semantics of EPCs: A Framework for Resolving the Vicious Circle. In: Desel, J.; Pernici, B.; Weske, M. (eds.): International Conference on Business Process Management (BPM 2004). Volume 3080 of Lecture Notes in Computer Science. Berlin et al. 2004, pp. 82-97.

[Kind06] Kindler, E.: On the semantics of EPCs: Resolving the vicious circle. Data & Knowledge Engineering, 56 (2006) 1, pp. 23-40.

[Mil80] Milner, R.: A Calculus of Communicating Systems. Volume 92 of Lecture Notes in Computer Science. Berlin et al. 1980.

[MRRA05] Mendling, J.; Recker, J.; Rosemann, M.; van der Aalst, W. M. P.: Towards the Interchange of Configurable EPCs: An XML-based Approach for Reference Model Configuration. In: Desel, J.; Frank, U. (eds.): Workshop on Enterprise Modelling and Information Systems Architectures (EMISA 2005). Volume 75 of Lecture Notes in Informatics. Bonn 2005, pp. 8-21.

[OwRa03] Owen, M.; Raj, J.: BPMN and Business Process Management – Introduction to the New Business Process Modeling Standard. Technical report, Popkin Software 2003.

[RDBS02] Rickayzen, A.; Dart, J.; Brennecke, C.; Schneider, M.: Practical Workflow for SAP: Effective Business Processes using SAP's WebFlow Engine. Bonn 2002.

[RoAa05] Rosemann, M.; van der Aalst, W. M. P.: A Configurable Reference Modelling Language. To appear in: Information Systems 2005.

[RoSc97] Rosemann, M.; Schütte, R.: Entwicklungsstand und Entwicklungsperspektiven der Referenzmodellierung. Arbeitsbericht 52 des Instituts für Wirtschaftsinformatik. Münster 1997.

[Rose03] Rosemann, M.: Application Reference Models and Building Blocks for Management and Control (ERP Systems). In: Bernus, P.; Nemes, L.; Schmidt, G. (eds.): Handbook on Enterprise Architecture. Berlin et al. 2003, pp. 596-616.

[Rose96] Rosemann, M.: Komplexitätsmanagement in Prozessmodellen: Methodenspezifische Gestaltungsempfehlungen für die Informationsmodellierung. Wiesbaden 1996.

[Sche00] Scheer, A.-W.: ARIS: Business Process Modelling. Berlin et al. 2000.

[Sche94] Scheer, A.-W.: Business Process Engineering. Reference Models for Industrial Enterprises. Berlin et al. 1994.

[Schü98] Schütte, R.: Grundsätze ordnungsmäßiger Referenzmodellierung. Konstruktion konfigurations- und anpassungsorientierter Modelle. Wiesbaden 1998.

[Schw99] Schwegmann, A.: Objektorientierte Referenzmodellierung. Theoretische Grundlagen und praktische Anwendung. Wiesbaden 1999.

[Staf00] Staffware: Staffware 2000 / GWD User Manual. Berkshire 2000.

# Supporting Enterprise Systems Introduction by Controlling-Enabled Configurative Reference Modeling

Tobias Rieke, Christian Seel

*Abstract: Enterprise system (ES) customization is often an expensive and time consuming task. These systems often come with preconfigured processes and data objects that can be regarded as best-practice and which are documented by information models. ES customization can be accelerated if these models are used for the customization process. This requires profound configuration and adaptation mechanisms together with a reference model that encompasses variants due to specific customer needs. To ensure continuous improvement towards a shorter customization time and reduced cost, controlling of the adaptation process becomes a crucial task. This controlling aims at improving the reference model basis and configuration mechanisms. Therefore we introduce configuration mechanisms that can be used to customize information models due to company characteristics in order to be interpreted afterwards by the ES to perform the necessary customization steps.*

## 1 Introduction and Related Work

### 1.1 Introduction

The introduction of comprehensive Enterprise Systems (ES) is often an expensive and time consuming task (cf. [Dave98]). In order to serve a preferably large market, ES vendors offer a lot of functionality in order to cope with a large amount of business requirements. The challenge is to align the business requirements of the regarded company with the provided functionality of the ES [Dave98; SoGD03]. Two strategies are possible: On the one hand, the enterprise introducing the ES can change its business processes in order to fit the functionality structure of the ES and to exploit the possible best practice solutions implemented in the ES. On the other hand, companies aim at adapting the ES to fit their business requirements, since comparative advantages due to special business processes of the companies are not influenced negatively. In most cases, a mixed strategy promises the best results.

As a consequence, two major tasks have to be fulfilled introducing an ES: First, business processes of the enterprise have to be reorganized in order to streamline them and make them fit to the ES. This affects not only processes to be implemented as ES functionality but also surrounding processes that are performed manually or serve as interfaces between employees and the ES respectively. Second, the ES has to be adapted to special requirements of the enterprise. Both tasks are related to extensive costs. For instance, the SAP system has over 3,000 configuration tables for customizing purposes [Dave98]. For this, specialized knowledge is needed which often results in severe consulting costs. Similarly, the reorganization of the surrounding business processes of the regarded company causes expenses spent on reorganization knowledge. Hence, in order to decrease these costs, a strategy is needed that allows an effective and efficient customizing of ES as well as an effective and efficient reorganization of surrounding business processes.

Detailed knowledge of ES customizing and business process reengineering can be stored in information models, since they are recognized as knowledge repositories [BDKK02]. In order to reduce ES introduction cost, special information models are needed that contain existent "best practice" or "common practice" knowledge [SoGD03]. These special information models are called reference models and can provide a basis for ES customization [SoGD03]. Nowadays, reference models are used for documentation purposes of ES and as a basis for business process change.

ES introduction can only be supported efficiently by reference models if the models can be easily adapted to specific application contexts – first in order to guarantee a proper fitness-for-use of the reference model according to the organizational needs of the company, and second in order to be able to perform the customizing process of the ES easily [SoGD03]. Manual adaptation of the models, and in turn, of the ES, could lead to economically non-justifiable adaptation efforts.

A continuous learning is necessary to improve the reference model adaptation accordingly their adaptation preciseness, the ease-of-use of the adaptation mechanisms, and the cost of the adaptation process. Thus, adaptation controlling is the next logical step to improve the reference model adaptation. Within this paper we present an approach to controlling-enabled configurative information modeling for ES introduction. First, we present related research in the next section. In chapter 2 we present the underlying research method. A procedure model for configurative reference modeling is proposed in chapter 3. In chapter 4, we introduce the utilization of configurative reference modeling by outlining examples based on Event-driven Process Chains (EPC, [Sche00]). In chapter 5, we reuse these examples in order to show how controlling concepts are used to assure the quality of the configuration process. Chapter 6 provides conclusions and predicted further research.

## 1.2 Related Research

In order to enable a context-specific adaptation of information models, few conceptual modeling approaches have been developed in the near past:

SOFFER ET AL. propose configurable information models in order to customize ES [SoGD03]. They use configurable, so-called Object-Process Diagrams that integrate process flows and data objects used within an ES. The configuration of these Object-Process Diagrams is performed by interpreting attributes that define the relation of diagram objects to different application scenarios. During ES customizing, the users have to specify their application context. Based on this, the attributes are interpreted, and the models are modified accordingly. The authors claim that it is necessary to connect model objects to particular ES functionality in order to guarantee an easy application of the proposed configuration approach.

ROSEMANN and VAN DER AALST propose a configurable reference modeling language that is based on EPCs [RoAa07]. The approach differs from that of SOFFER ET AL. in so far as configurations are less predefined. It is based on semantic patterns in process models that describe dependencies of model elements on a semantic basis. E. g., a manual model configuration step that erases a process branch is followed by a hint to erase another process branch as well that is semantically related to the prior one. Similarly to SOFFER ET AL., the authors point out the necessity to connect model elements to the according ES functions in order to perform a model and ES configuration concurrently.

The approach which has been introduced by BECKER ET AL. [BDKK02] is based on the view building approach "Architecture of Integrated Information Systems" (ARIS [Sche00]) in order to comply with different modeling views that are needed for the integrated modeling of ES and surrounding business processes. In comparison to the approaches of SOFFER ET AL. as well as ROSEMANN and VAN DER AALST, it is different inasmuch configuration techniques are provided that have different influences on the models. The approach provides a set of configuration mechanisms that are able to format modeling languages, models and model sections as well as model elements in order to fit to context specific requirements. Furthermore, the approach is not restricted to conceptual configurations of information models but allows also configurations of the graphical representation of models as well as the management of different languages and language-internal synonyms used in model element designations in different application scenarios. The introduction of ES is hence supported by automated model based configuration.

The configuration strategy of each of the introduced approaches is similar. Model variants for different application scenarios are integrated in one model and predefined. The model variant that is considered the best for a specific application scenario can be selected. Therefore, these approaches provide a useful contribution in model based ES and process configuration.

In this contribution, we use the approach of BECKER ET AL. as a basis for further controlling-related extensions. We chose this approach, first due to its greatest comprehension and second, due to the fact that it was developed "in-house" which allowed an in-depth pre-understanding of the approach.

## 2  Research Methodology

Our contribution consists of providing configuration methods that target Enterprise System configuration. The relevance of the research topic was derived from requirements the authors were confronted with during information model-driven consulting projects. These were performed amongst others at the *DeTe Immobilien GmbH* [BeKR05], in *public administrations of the German federal state of North Rhine-Westphalia* [BADN06], at *Bayer Business Services GmbH* [BJDF06], in the *German Federal Armed Forces* as well as in association with *itemis GmbH & Co. KG*. The requirements gathered within these consulting projects were balanced with already existing approaches to information model adaptation as briefly outlined in section 1.2, whereas a deficit of methodical support for this problem was identified.

Before presenting the reference modeling procedure framework it is necessary to constitute our epistemological background of this working paper. Therefore we will take position in an epistemological reference framework.

As a basis for the scientific philosophical positioning of this paper a reference framework will be used that was introduced by BECKER and NIEHAVES [BeNi07, p. 202]. It stresses five questions that are of relevance for the epistemological positioning (without abnegating further questions). Each question can be assigned to different positions. In the following, each question will be described and our position will be stressed and reasoned.

- *What is the artifact of cognition (ontological aspect)?* Ontology is the science, the theory or the analysis of to be, the exploration of "what is" and "how it is" [Foer96]. This paper is founded on the position of *onto-logical realism*. This means, researchers are making the assumption that a real world exists, independent from the human awareness [Bung77].

- *How is the relation between cognition and the artifact of cognition? (epistemological aspect)?* The main questions in epistemology, about the relation between the acquired cognition of the subject and the arti-fact of cognition, want to answer if artifacts outside the human thinking and speaking can be objectively recognized. The epistemological posi-tion of this paper pronounces the influence of the subject [Glas87; Lore87]. We assume that cognition is mediated by the subject. There-fore we follow the epistemological position of *constructivism* and in particular – according to our ontological realistic position – *interpretiv-ism* [BuMo79; KlMy99]. The consequence is that the intersubjective mediation of model conclusions is founded on the use of a shared termi-nology between the researchers. Thus, we confer to KAMLAH and LO-RENZEN who point out that a shared terminology within a community can be systematically developed [KaLo96]. Concerning the method pre-sented in this paper, it is necessary for the understanding of the different individuals that are dealing with the reference model configuration and succeeding adaptation process, to integrate constructs for creation of standardized terms. This can be achieved e. g. by the construction of a terminology or glossary [Spie93].

- *What is true cognition?* The question, how the human can achieve "true" cognition, aims at the question, whether "true" knowledge can be achieved and what is the process to test the truth of knowledge. Con-cerning the development and evaluation of modeling techniques and procedure models as well as the verification of information out of refer-ence models and reorganization recommendations the concept of truth builds the major benchmark. This paper is oriented to the *consensus theory* of truth [Habe73] We assume that truth emerges from the con-sensus of a competent language community. This consensus building community consists of experts who find consensus through "interper-sonal verification" [KaLo96]. For the verification of the method intro-duced in this paper and the information contained in reference models as well as reorganization recommendations, methods like observation, in-terviews and interpretation of texts can be used. Besides, we adopt the finding of TARSKI that truth is always related to a language – the so called object language. This requires the existence of a meta language that contains truth predicates about the statements of the object language [Tars44].

- *Where does cognition come from (source of cognition)?* The question after the source of cognition deals with the positions of the fundamental ability of cognition. The findings of this paper are achieved by reflection of the method and model contents as well as their application. Therefore, we follow KANT'S position who states that both "a priori" knowledge (rationalism [Leib62; Chom65]) as well as "a posteriori" (empiricism [Hume84; Quin61]) knowledge acquisition is necessary in scientific processes [Kant99].

- *How does cognition emerge (methodological aspect)?* The methodological aspect of epistemology deals with the question, how cognition can be achieved. In this paper we are using *deductive* [Lore95] and *inductive* [Rott95; Seif96] conclusions. If a single conclusion can be generalized on the basis of a group of single verifications, an inductive conclusion has been made. In the case of reference model construction a deductive conclusion is also possible. This is the case if model elements are assigned to specific object categories by category-specific attributes. Also in the field of verification of truth deductive procedures (decomposition of complex model conclusion to single conclusion) as well as inductive procedures (generalization of various single conclusions) are necessary.

## 3  Reference Modeling Life Cycle

Reference models that reflect best practice or state of the art, are affected by changes like the companies they describe. These changes arise from actual technological or organizational developments. Thus, reference model developers must deal with learning issues. Organizational learning can be distinguished in single loop and double loop learning [ArSc74]. Single loop learning deals with the optimization (error elimination) e. g. of a process by keeping the original process goals and assumptions. Double loop learning takes the assumptions into consideration and therefore can result in a completely new aligned process striving for new goals.

According to known life cycle models from the field of process management [GaSc95], controlling [BaCG99], and risk management [JuKr03], the *reference modeling life cycle* deals with learning issues starting with the initial development of the reference model, its adaptation process, leading to the usage of the underlying ES, and ending in a feedback (cf. Figure 1). Within this cycle two different parties are involved: the reference model developer (ES vendor) and the reference model user (ES customer). The phases of the reference model life cycle are described in the following ([BDKK02, pp. 34ff.] discuss a similar reference modeling cycle).

## 3.1 Requirements Definition

The goal of our reference modeling approach is to provide customization support for ES. Information models perform the task of representing problems in their current processing state. They provide solution contributions to a development problem [NeSi72]. The quality of a model is the better the more it complies with the subjective model resulting from the user-specific perspective on the problem situation [DaSh96; Rose98; RoSD05]. Within this phase, different configuration parameters have to be distinguished (cf. section 4.1) which supports different views on the model [BDKK02, pp. 27ff.]. In addition, the flexibility of the customization process has to be determined whether it should allow higher degrees of freedom regarding the model adaptation besides configuration mechanisms whose possible outcome is determined in advance (cf. section 5).

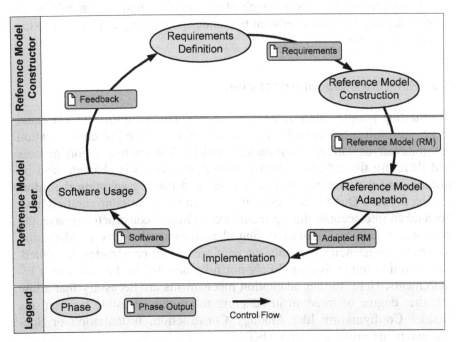

**Figure 1:** Reference Modeling Life Cycle

## 3.2 Reference Model Construction

The various aspects that are object of ES customization have to be represented within information models. Usually this primarily leads to process and data models. In the first run of the cycle the modeling language has to be selected. In a further cycle an adaptation of the modeling language can become necessary. The language should be adequate regarding the modeling artifacts and the user requirements and skills.

The construction of the different models is driven by the configuration parameters that have been identified within the previous requirements phase. Every information model has to be verified whether a certain configuration parameter is of relevance to the model. If a parameter leads to an adaptation, a variant has to be defined within the model (the mechanisms of variant definition are described in chapter 5). Moreover, the support of different configuration parameters leads to either additional aspects that have to be defined, or the absence of specific model elements that are not in the scope of the configuration parameter targeted ES. Due to the fact that the configuration parameters are of relevance to all models, keeping the consistency of the whole bunch of information models– especially regarding the dependencies between the models – is a very crucial task to the model constructor.

## 3.3  Reference Model Adaptation

The starting point of the reference model adaptation (in this context equal to ES customization) is an ES provided with a modeling or customization environment containing information models. The customization process and therefore the reference model adaptation process is characterized by instantiating the configuration parameters and thereby adapting the information models. Due to the fact, that the possibilities of configuration have been taken into account during the reference model construction phase, the consistency can be assured during the configuration-driven adaptation phase. Inconsistencies can only occur if the model constructor has failed. The resulting model is most likely not fully adapted to the customer's requirements. Here, further adaptation mechanisms are necessary that allow a higher degree of freedom in adapting the model. Possible mechanisms besides Configuration like Analogy Construction, Instantiation or Specialization are presented in [BeDK04].

## 3.4  Implementation

The implementation phase within the customization process can be regarded as the translation or even transformation of the adapted (reference) model into the thereby specified software. Therefore e. g. tables have to be adapted, data sets have to be initialized, workflows have to be configured and interfaces have to be offered. These steps are performed by routines that are provided with the ES. An approach which has been discussed lately in the literature is the Model-driven Architecture (MDA) [KlWB03; HaPo03]. Within this approach software is implemented by transforming information models into more specific ones and at last into the running software (from platform-independent model to platform-specific model to code). This is achieved by providing generators which can enrich the model with more detailed information. Information models – discussed in this paper – can be used as a starting point to a MDA transformation.

## 3.5  Software Usage

After the ES has been customized, the ES is ready for use. But before the ES can go live, testing and simulation steps are advisable. During these steps and the following live usage of the ES shortcomings of the customization process can occur and be identified. In this case, the cycle has to be reinitiated starting with the requirements phase. According to the Rational Unified Process [Kruc04] the amount of corrections decreases and its focus is moving towards the software usage phase with each cycle.

Although, all shortcomings are addressed that might have occurred during the reference process life cycle, further cycles become necessary during the ongoing use of the software due to the changing environment and business.

## 4  Configurative Reference Modeling

In order to provide efficient adaptation support, configurable reference models comprise rules which allow modifications of the original reference model depending on company or project individual determinations of configuration parameters.

## 4.1  Configuration Parameters

When used in order to construct a specific information model, reference models have to be adapted to company or project specific issues. Starting from the factors describing information model application contexts already introduced in chapter 3, we distinguish the following parameters that a reference model configuration depends on:

*Business characteristics* and their *values* represent sets of companies for which a reference model adaptation shall be performed. E. g., business characteristics are the performed business type or the trade level. Exemplary trade-related values of the business type are warehousing, third-party-deal and central settlement; values of trade level are e. g. whole trade and retail trade [BeSc04, pp. 2, 74].

*Perspectives* represent information model requirements of different user groups. Perspectives are determined by the modeling purpose (e. g. ES customizing or process oriented organizational design), the organizational role of the actual user (e. g. manager, method expert or accounting clerk) and further influences like individual preferences according to the graphical design of the models [BDKK02, pp. 28ff.].

## 4.2  Model Projection

The most significant problem that results from a multiplicity of context specific variants is the need to manage possible redundancies inside the model itself. This leads to increased modeling and maintenance cost as well as the danger of inconsistencies within the model base. In the case of business process redesign, inconsistencies lead to a reduced applicability (e. g. for training), in the case of ES customizing, inconsistencies can even cause malfunctions of the software system.

In order to enable an efficient model construction and model maintenance, redundancies have to be overcome. A modeling language which enables users to avoid redundancies and to consider multiple variants within the model base is called configurative reference modeling (for the following cf. [BDKK02, p. 26]). The approach is based on the concept of model projection. A configurable model that provides all relevant information for each variant contains constraints that determine to which variant each model element belongs. By this means redundancies are avoided and, simultaneously, modeling of multiple application contexts is made possible. When a configuration is performed, each model element is hidden that does not belong to the selected variant.

## 4.3  Configuration Mechanisms Overview

In order to support the reference model user by model projection efficiently, it is beneficial to supply model projection based configuration mechanisms that have different impacts on the models. Therefore, configuration mechanisms are not exclusively proposed for the layer of modeling

technique application (model layer), but also for the layer of their definition (meta-model layer). Configurative adaptations of meta-models act
upon all models which were constructed in the corresponding modeling
language, whereas adaptations on model layer only act upon specific models and model sections respectively.

In the following, we present examples of model configurations based on
Event-Driven Process Chains with different configuration mechanisms (for
a detailed conceptual introduction cf. [BDKK02, pp. 72ff.]). We distinguish the following configuration mechanisms:

- Model Type Selection
- Element Type Selection
- Element Selection
- Synonym Management
- Representation Variation

Within this paper, we focus on the Model Type and Element Type Selection as well as Element Selection. Synonym Management and Representation Variation do not play a crucial role within the adaptation controlling.

### *Model Type Selection*

Model Type Selection considers the perspective-specific relevance of
model types which applies especially for organizational change projects.
Model types represent the application types of modeling techniques, which
can be combined in the context of reference modeling techniques, e. g.
Event-Driven Process Chains (EPC) [Sche00], Entity Relationship Models
(ERM) [Chen76], technical term models [Spie93] or organizational charts.
The configuration mechanism assigns perspectives to model types and supports a coarse configuration of the model system. The model types, which
are not relevant for the model user's perspective, are hidden.

### *Element Type Selection*

Finer configuration rules existing on meta-model layer can be performed
by using Element Type Selection (cf. the corresponding meta-meta model
in Figure 2). Model types are characterized by the element types which are
assigned to them and their relations among each other. In case of the EPC,
these are e. g. functions, events, and resources. The configuration mechanism admits to create variants of model types by assigning element types
to perspectives and, if necessary, by fading them out. E. g., variants of
EPC differ in model element types which are annotatable to functions.
Candidates for annotations are e. g. entity types, application systems and
organizational units. The use of different types of the EPC takes place es-

pecially in reorganization projects. The model type variants are created by assigning element types to them which shall be faded out. Each model type variant is assigned to one or more perspectives.

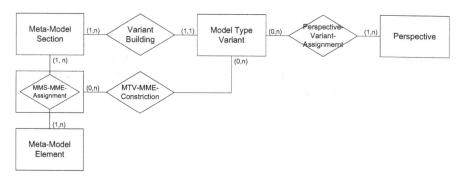

**Figure 2:** Meta-meta model constructs for Element Type Selection

## *Element Selection*

Element Selection permits the selection of single elements on model layer. There are different criteria for Element Selection which differ in the type of definition of the favored element subset:

*Element Selection via attributes*: The creation of variants by Element Selection via attributes is achieved by analyzing the characteristics which are assigned to the reference model elements. An attribute, for example, can be intended for the functions of an EPC for the identification of its automation degree (cf. Figure 3).

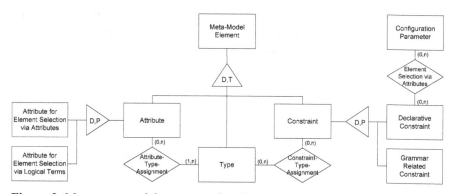

**Figure 3:** Meta-meta model constructs for Element Selection

*Element Selection via logical terms*: The Element Selection via attributes becomes inefficient as soon as the number of newly to be introduced attributes reaches a high level. Therefore the configuration mechanism of Element Selection via logical terms is additionally introduced, which enables to assign model elements directly to configuration parameter values by using a logical term. The annotation of an expression, e. g. "perspective (organizational design)", to a model element flags the regarded element as relevant only for the perspective organizational design (cf. the corresponding specifications in Figure 3 and Figure 4). The utilization of Element Selection via attributes can be recommended alternatively, only if already considered attributes of elements can be reused.

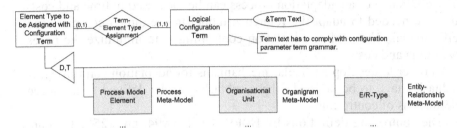

**Figure 4:** Meta-model constructs for Element Selection via logical terms

Element Selections are considered to be relevant both for ES customizing and business process reengineering. First, Element Selection allows omitting specific model sections which leads to exclude (or hide) specific parts of the ES functionality. Second, the omission of model sections in business process reengineering hides information that is not relevant for specific user groups within the project, e. g. organizational designers in specific branch offices in which only parts of the whole business are performed (e. g. retail branch offices of a wholesaler).

| | |
|---|---|
| \<Logical Term\> | ::= \<Expression\> {\<Operator\> \<Expression\>} |
| \<Expression\> | ::= \<Prefix\> "Perspective" |
| | \<Perspective Value List\> |
| \<Expression\> | ::= \<Prefix\> \<Business Characteristic\> |
| | \<Business Characteristic Value List\> |
| \<Perspective Value List\> | ::= "(" \<Prefix\> \<Perspective Value List\> |
| | { \<Operator\> \<Prefix\> \<Perspective Value List\> } ")" |
| \<Perspective Value List\> | ::= \<Perspective\> |
| \<Business Characteristic Value List\> | ::= "(" \<Prefix\> \<Business Characteristic Value List\> |
| | { \<Operator\> \<Prefix\> \<Business Characteristic Value List\> } ")" |
| \<Business Characteristic Value List\> | ::= \<Business Characteristic Value\> |
| \<Operator\> | ::= "\|" \| "+" |
| \<Prefix\> | ::= "NOT" \| \<empty\> |

**Figure 5:** Extract from the grammar for Element Selection via logical terms

In case of Element Selection via logical terms, the relevance of a model element for a selected configuration depends on a logical term which is assigned to the element. In this context logical terms are understood as special attributes that can be assigned to model elements. They describe directly in which configuration the respective model element is available. Terms have to comply with a predefined grammar (cf. Figure 5) for analysis purposes.

## 5 Adaptation Controlling

The efficiency of an adaptation process can be measured in time and costs, that are needed to adapt the reference model to the aimed company-specific model. The goal of adaptation controlling is to minimize the necessary time and costs.

In order to develop particular mechanisms for adaptation controlling, its subtasks have to be defined. These subtasks can be derived from current definitions of controlling.

The controlling definitions by HORVÁTH [Horv94, pp. 125f., 144] and REICHMANN [Reic95] focus on the three controlling subtasks *planning*, *control* and *coordination*. Related to the goal of adaptation controlling, controlling mechanisms support the planning by providing proper adaptations for specific requirements. The subtask control is addressed by checking whether the specified requirements to the specific model are fulfilled after the adaptation process. The subtask coordination is less important for the controlling of adaptive reference models.

A direction how adaptation controlling can be achieved is provided by ZIEGENBEIN [Zieg04, pp. 23], who expresses that controlling has to develop suitable methods to support its three subtasks. GROB [Grob96, pp. 137-158] refines this by depicting two major tasks of controlling: (1) creation and maintenance of an infrastructure for information provision in order to support planning and control (system design) and (2) coordination und execution of planning and control (system usage).

These definitions imply for the controlling of adaptive reference models, that an information infrastructure for planning and control and a concept for its usage have to be developed. The necessity for that has already been recognized [Schü98, pp. 300-308; OtKl99, pp. 23-29] but an operationalized concept is still missing. Therefore we first introduce the extended reference model cycle that describes the necessary steps for a reference model adaptation controlling. Then we describe the mechanisms and meta-model extensions that are necessary to perform an efficient model feedback and controlling.

## 5.1 Feedback Cycles in the Procedure Model

To minimize the effort that is necessary to adapt the reference model to a customer-specific model, the controlling phase strives for the goal to identify shortcomings and possible improvements of the reference model and its adaptation mechanisms.

The adaptation controlling phase is best positioned within the reference modeling cycle between software usage and requirements engineering (cf. Figure 6), where first attempts of controlling exist with an unstructured feedback resulting from the experience with the software (cf. Figure 1).

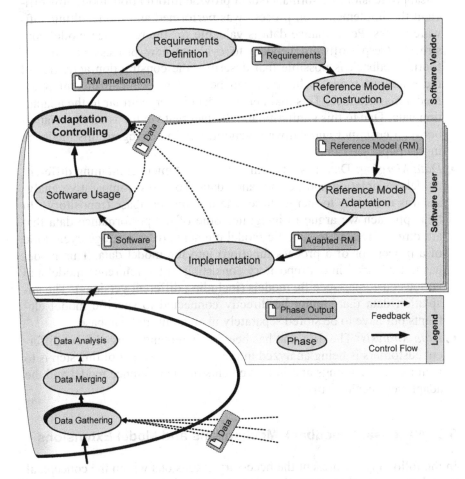

**Figure 6:** Reference Modeling Life Cycle with controlling phase

The controlling phase can be structured in a sequence of three consecutive steps:

- *Data Gathering:* The data that is gathered throughout the customization process can be differentiated in model data, adaptation data and performance data. *Model data* mainly consists of the final adapted model resulting from the adaptation process. *Adaptation data* describes the process of adaptation and delivers information about the time that was spend on adapting the model, the order in which the adaptation was performed and e. g. the configuration steps that had to be refined due to misapprehension. Performance data provide information about how efficient the implementation process was performed and the resulting software works. Performance data is valuable for the reference model constructor (resp. software vendor) to evaluate new process variants. A fourth feedback is possible that describes the construction activities of the reference model. This data can be used to evaluate the reference model maintenance. This maintenance data is very similar to the adaptation data. Due to this similarity and the fact that we focus on the relation between customer and software vendor, we do not regard this feedback in this paper later on.
- *Data Merging:* Data is sent from various customers containing different models, adaptation and performance data. To allow comparative analyses it is necessary to merge these data into one database (repository). In this approach we argue to integrate some of the performance data that are directly related to specific model elements (e. g. average cycle time of a process or of a process function) into the model data. This model has to be loaded into a repository consisting of the reference model and various customer-specific models (including different versions). The adaptation data that cannot be directly connected to specific model elements but have to be stored separately in an audit trail database.
- *Data Analysis:* The data that has been gathered and merged from different customers is being analyzed in the third step. Target of this step is to identify shortcomings and improvements of the reference model and the adaptation mechanisms.

## 5.2 Necessary Feedback Mechanisms and Model Extensions

In the following we present the necessary extensions within the conceptual model to enable the controlling and model maintenance. Therefore, as a key mechanism, it is necessary to retrieve the customer's model out of the model repository, which stores all customer-specific models together and integrated with the reference model. Using the configurative approach a customer-specific perspective has to be defined. The configuration mechanisms presented in chapter 4 do not allow for selecting all the necessary model elements to show the customer-specific model. For instance, attributes can not be assigned to a specific customer because they do not have attributes of their own. Therefore, we introduce a new configuration mechanism, which selects model elements' properties (cf. also in the following Figure 7). Properties (as some kind of meta data) should be assigned to all model elements. Thus, it is possible to assign a customer to an attribute or a constraint. In this case, we define properties as data that are not part of the model itself but are needed for maintenance reasons (e. g. date of creation, name of the creator, version ID etc.). To ensure the selection (Element Selection by properties), the *configuration parameter*, e. g. a customer perspective, has to be assigned to the *property type*.

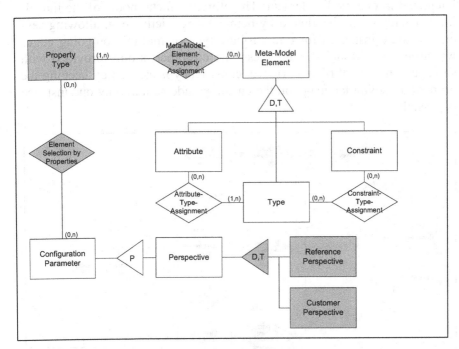

**Figure 7:** Meta-meta model extensions for Element Selection by properties

To provide data for controlling purposes the conceptual model has to be extended to describe the controlling relevant data and distinguish the user-specific model. As an important precondition, every model element has to be identified regarding its source in the reference model. Therefore it is necessary to provide a valid identifier (property type: ID) for each model element (attributes, types, and constraints). This also allows identifying the model elements that has been omitted or additionally added. Therefore the modeling environment must support the generation of unique IDs throughout all modeling environments. The ID must not be mistaken for the unique ID (primary key) provided by the database to distinguish the table entries. The ID described in this paragraph identifies the model element that can exist in various variants throughout different customers. All these variants share the same ID. Thus, for the ES vendor it has a grouping character, grouping all variants.

All Elements, uploaded by the customer, have to be recognized in the customer's perspective. This can be achieved during the upload phase where the customer identifies himself by initiating the upload session. Every uploaded model element is assigned to the customer (property type: Customer). This also allows having customer-specific attribute instances integrated in one model element. Therefore the meta model of the modeling language has to be altered by being less restrictive e. g. allowing several attribute instances for one attribute type or multiple outgoing edges within an EPC-Model. Nevertheless, the customer is only provided with single and unique attributes. Hence, consistency is assured by keeping the original modeling language on the customer side so that only one instance is possible.

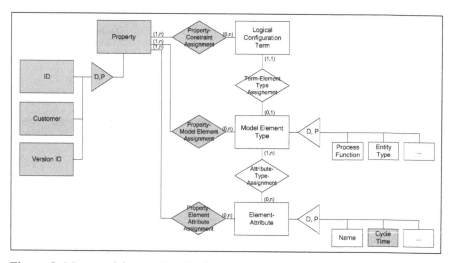

**Figure 8:** Meta model extension for data gathering

The nature of a cycle is that every step is performed not only once. Therefore the model must ensure that the customer is able to upload an advanced model later on. This requires properties for versioning. Every model element that has been uploaded is assigned to customer-specific version ID identifying the model elements that are part of a version. Model elements that have not been changed are additionally assigned to the new version.

Performance data can be integrated into the customer-specific model as attributes in the customer's adapted model. But this is only possible for data that is standardized and comparable. To provide performance data e. g. of single process instances an audit trail is the best solution. In order to provide a reference from the performance data to the model element to which it is connected the audit trail has to provide a field for this assignment. The reference data that can be provided with the model should give performance information like the average cycle time for a process or a process function. Within the conceptual model on the meta-model layer the element attribute has to be specialized in the types (e. g. cycle time) that should be provided by the customer. The resulting meta-model is depicted in Figure 8:

An example of the integration of two customer-specific models is depicted in Figure 9. This Figure describes two processes (defined as an EPC). The process of customer B is extended due to a control step. During the data merging phase, corresponding model elements are identified with use of their ID (not depicted in the figure). Equal model elements are assigned to the entry of the Property Customer A and B (also not depicted in the figure, due to readability). New model elements are only assigned to their corresponding customer.

## 5.3  Privacy Complaints

In practical use the exchange of data between the customer and ES vendor as described above is a highly relevant action for security issues. As this is crucial information about an enterprise, which should not be accessible for competitors, a privacy concept has been developed. This concept provides different levels of feedback details, which allows an enterprise to decide how much information the reference model creator receives.

The *first level* is the most secure one and just provides no feedback. The *second level* provides only the configuration parameters that were chosen by the customer. No additional data despite the configuration parameters are transferred. Thus, important and often used, but preconfigured variants can be determined. Within a *third level* the fully adapted model is uploaded, which allows to encounter new variants and identify shortcomings of existing variants in comparison to other models from different customers. In a *further level* performance data and/or adaptation can be provided.

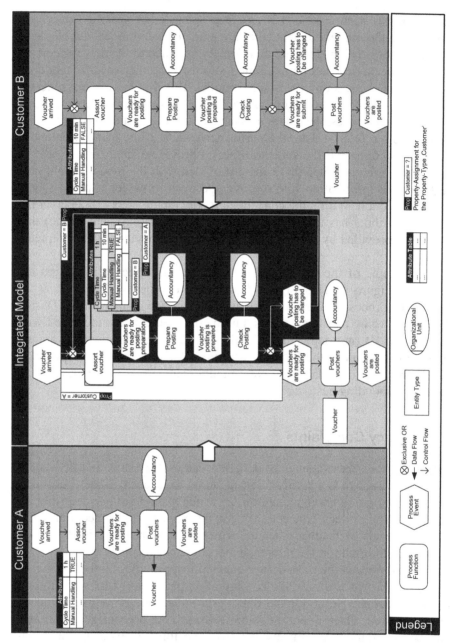

**Figure 9:** Integration example of two customer-specific models

Performance data provide highly relevant information about the evaluation of variants. They can possibly serve as an advisor during the adaptation phase by providing a reference benchmark.

## 6 Conclusions and Further Research

It has been shown how the adaptation controlling of conceptual reference models to specific application contexts can be supported comprehensively. Therefore, recommendations for the construction of reference modeling languages in terms of configuration mechanisms have been formulated.

The conceptual specifications of the configuration mechanisms can be used as a basis for the implementation of modeling tools that are able to support configurative reference modeling. Because of the extensive complexity of configurable reference models that results from the integrated configuration rules, the support by modeling tools is a necessary precondition for the application of configurative reference modeling in practice. Handling configurable reference models with common draft applications is – in case of realistic project volumes – considered to be impossible due to acceptance and cost barriers. Hence our further research and development work focuses at implementing configurative reference modeling as a plug-in for a well-known modeling tool. Additionally, the plug-in will be used as a basis for the evaluation of the proposed configuration mechanisms in practical fieldwork.

Furthermore, not only the configuration mechanisms themselves have to be implemented and evaluated. But also the controlling steps require system support. Therefore we provided extensions of a conceptual model for configurative reference modeling for controlling purposes, which allow revealing potential improvements of the reference model adaptation process and the adaptive reference model itself. As these controlling concepts require the transfer of maybe crucial information, information security was taken into account. Despite of this security level approach the reference model improvement is the more successful the more information and especially the more manual adjusted models are available. So a future task is the development of incentives that make it attractive for the user to submit information to the ES vendor. E. g., free updates can serve as such an incentive. Additionally, other controlling steps have to be regarded in more detail, such as analyzing the new model repository and deriving potential for improving the model and the adaptation technique.

## References


[ArSc74] Argyris, C.; Schön, D.: Theory in practice: Increasing professional effectiveness. San Francisco 1974.

[BaCG99] Baum, H.-G.; Coenenberg, A.; Günther, T.: Strategisches Controlling. 2nd edition, Stuttgart 1999.

[BADN06] Becker, J.; Algermissen, L.; Delfmann, P.; Niehaves, B.: Configurable Reference Process Models for Public Administrations. In: Anttiroiki, A.-V.; Mälkiä, M. (Eds.): Encyclopedia of Digital Government. Hershey et al. 2006, pp. 220-223.

[BDKK02] Becker, J.; Delfmann, P.; Knackstedt, K.; Kuropka, K.: Konfigurative Referenzmodellierung. In: Becker, J.; Knackstedt, R. (Eds.): Wissensmanagement mit Referenzmodellen. Konzepte für die Anwendungssystem- und Organisationsgestaltung. Heidelberg 2002, S. 25-144.

[BeDK04] Becker, J.; Delfmann, P.; Knackstedt, R.: Konstruktion von Referenzmodellierungssprachen. Ein Ordnungsrahmen zur Spezifikation von Adaptionsmechanismen für Informationsmodelle. Wirtschaftsinformatik 46 (2004) 4, S. 251-264.

[BeKR05] Becker, J.; Kugeler, M.; Rosemann, M. (Eds.): Prozessmanagement. Ein Leitfaden zur prozessorientierten Organisationsgestaltung. 5th edition, Berlin et al. 2005.

[BeNi07] Becker, J.; Niehaves, B.: Epistemological Perspectives on IS Research – A Framework for Analyzing and Systematizing Epistemological Assumptions. Information Systems Journal, Special Issue on Philosophy and Epistemology in IS. 2007.

[BeSc04] Becker, J.; Schütte, R.: Handelsinformationssysteme. 2nd edition, Frankfurt am Main 2004.

[BJDF06] Becker, J.; Janiesch, C.; Delfmann, P.; Fuhr, W.: Perspectives on Process Documentation – A Case Study. In: Chen, C.-S.; Filipe, J.; Seruca, I.; Cordeiro, J. (Eds.): Enterprise Information Systems VII. Dordrecht 2006, pp. 167-177.

[BuMo79] Burrell, G.; Morgan, G.: Sociological Paradigms and Organisational Anlysis: Elements of the Sociology of Corporate Life. Brookfield 1979.

[Bung77] Bunge, M. A.: Ontology I: The Furniture of the World. Treatise on Basic Philosophy. Dordrecht 1977.

[Chen76] Chen, P. P.: The Entity-Relationship Model. Toward a Unified View of Data. ACM Transactions on Database-Systems 1 (1976) 1, pp. 9-36.

[Chom65] Chomsky, N.: Aspects of the Theory of Syntax. Cambridge 1965.

[DaSh96] Darke, P.; Shanks, G.: Stakeholder Viewpoints in Requirements Definition. Requirements Engineering 1 (1996) 1, pp. 88-105.

[Dave98] Davenport, T.: Putting the enterprise into the enterprise system. Harvard Business Review 76 (1998) 4, pp. 121-131.

[Foer96] von Foerster, H.: Wissen und Gewissen. Versuch einer Brücke. 4th edition, Frankfurt am Main 1996.

[GaSc95] Galler, J.; Scheer, A.-W.: Workflow-Projekte: Vom Geschäftsprozeß zur unternehmensspezifischen Workflow-Anwendung. Information Management 10 (1995) 1, S. 20-28.

[Glas87] von Glasersfeld, E.: The Construction of Knowledge. Seaside 1987.

[Grob96] Grob, H. L.: Positionsbestimmung des Controlling. In: Scheer, A.-W. (Hrsg.): Rechnungswesen und EDV: Kundenorientierung in Industrie, Dienstleistung und Verwaltung. Heidelberg 1996, pp. 137-158.

[Habe73] Habermas, J.: Wahrheitstheorien. In: Fahrenbach, H. (Hrsg.): Wirklichkeit und Reflexion. Walter Schulz zum 60. Geburtstag. Pfullingen 1973, pp. 211-265.

[HaPo03] Halmans, G.; Pohl, K.: Communicating the Variability of a Software-Product Family to Customers. Software and System Modeling 2 (2003) 1, pp. 15-36.

[Horv94] Horváth, P.: Controlling. 5th edition. Munich 1994.

[Hume84] Hume, D.: Eine Untersuchung über den menschlichen Verstand. Ditzingen 1984.

[JuKr03] Junginger, M.; Krcmar, H.: Risikomanagement im Informationsmanagement – Eine spezifische Aufgabe des IV-Controllings. Information Management & Consulting, 18 (2003) 2 pp. 16-23.

[KaLo96] Kamlah, W.; Lorenzen, P.: Logische Propädeutik: Vorschule des vernünftigen Redens. Stuttgart, Weimar 1996.

[Kant99] Kant, I.: Critique of Pure Reason. Cambridge 1999.

[KlMy99] Klein, H. K.; Myers, M. D.: A Set of Principles for Conducting and Evaluating Interpretive Field Studies in Information Systems. MIS Quarterly 23 (1999) 1, pp. 67-93.

[KlWB03] Kleppe, A.; Warmer, J.; Bast, W.: MDA Explained: The Model Driven Architecture – Practice and Promise. Boston et al. 2003.

[Kruc04] Kruchten, P.: The Rational Unified Process. 2nd edition, Boston et al. 2004.

[Leib62] Leibniz, G.-W.: Nouveaux Essais sur l'Entendement Humain. In: Leibniz, G.-W. (ed.): Sämtliche Schriften. Berlin 1962, pp. 39-527.

[Lore87] Lorenzen, P.: Constructive Philosophy. Amherst 1987.

[Lore95] Lorenz, K.: Deduktion. In: Mittelstraß, J. (Ed.): Enzyklopädie Philosophie und Wissenschaftstheorie. Issue 1. Stuttgart, Weimar 1995, p. 434.

[NeSi72] Newell, A.; Simon, H.A.: Human problem solving. 2nd edition, Englewood Cliffs 1972.

[OtKl99] Otto, A.; Klaus, P.: Referenzmodelle als Basis des Benchmarkings. io management 68 (1999) 4.

[Quin61] Quine, W. V. O.: Two Dogmas of Empiricism. In: Quine, W. V. O. (Hrsg.): From a Logical Point of View. Cambridge 1961, pp. 20-46.

[Reic95] Reichmann, T.: Controlling mit Kennzahlen und Managementberichten: Grundlagen einer systemgestützten Controlling-Konzeption. 4th edition, Munich 1995.

[RoAa07] Rosemann, M.; van der Aalst, W. M. P.: A Configurable Reference Modelling Language. Information Systems 23 (2007) 1, S. 1-23.

[RoSD05] Rosemann, M.; Schwegmann, A.; Delfmann, P.: Vorbereitung der Prozessmodellierung. In: Becker, J.; Kugeler, M.; Rosemann, M. (Eds.): Prozessmanagement. Ein Leitfaden zur prozessorientierten Organisationsgestaltung. 5th edition, Berlin et al. 2005, pp. 45-103.

[Rose98] Rosemann, M.: Managing the Complexity of Multiperspective Information Models using the Guidelines of Modeling. In: Fowler, D.; Dawson, L. (Eds.): Proceedings of the 3rd Australian Conference on Requirements Engineering. Geelong 1998, pp. 101-118.

[Rott95] Rott, H.: Schluß, induktiver. In: Mittelstraß, J. (Ed.): Enzyklopädie Philosophie und Wissenschaftstheorie 3. Stuttgart, Weimar 1995, pp. 710-713.

[Sche00] Scheer, A.-W.: ARIS – Business Process Modeling. 3rd edition. Berlin et al. 2000.

[Schü98] Schütte, R.: Grundsätze ordnungsmäßiger Referenzmodellierung. Wiesbaden 1998.

[Seif96] Seiffert, H.: Einführung in die Wissenschaftstheorie 1. 12th edition, Munich 1996.

[SoGD03] Soffer, P.; Golany, B.; Dori, D.: ERP modeling: a comprehensive approach. Information Systems 28 (2003) 9, pp 673-690.

[Spie93] Spiegel, H.: Methodik zur Analyse und Dokumentation fachlicher Begriffswelten innerhalb des Unternehmens TELEKOM. Darmstadt 1993.

[Tars44] Tarski, A.: The Semantic Concept of Truth and the foundation of semantics. Philosophy and Phenomenological Research 4 (1944) 3, pp. 341-375.

[Zieg04] Ziegenbein, K.: Controlling. 8th edition, Ludwigshafen 2004.

# RefMod<sup>PM</sup>: Reference Information Model for Enterprise-Wide Project Planning, Controlling and Coordination in Matrix Project Organizations

Frederik Ahlemann

*Abstract: Project information systems can be regarded as a sub-system of project management systems. Their aim is to supply all relevant stakeholders with the information necessary to plan, control and coordinate projects. The objective of the research presented in this paper is the development of a semi-formal, conceptual reference information model for the enterprise-wide planning, controlling and coordination of projects in matrix project organizations, which can serve as a basis for information system development (RefMod<sup>PM</sup>). The reference model construction is based on 13 in-depth interviews with domain experts from large German and Swiss enterprises and the analysis of 28 commercial software products for the problem domain. The paper reflects the corresponding research process and shows the reference model's architecture. Parts of the reference model are discussed to give an impression of the outcome of the research.*

## 1    Introduction

Due to increasing changes in today's environment, enterprises are facing a constant need for the development of new or the adaptation of existing processes, organizational structures and products [Peri93, pp. 30-79; Vahs99, p. 9]. Such innovations are typically implemented with the help of projects. As a result, projects have become a vital part of today's business life [Gesc93, pp. 11-22]. They are widely regarded as building blocks for implementing business strategies and for maintaining an enterprise's competitiveness [Turn99, pp. 35-48; Sche04]. At the same time, project work is no longer restricted to R&D activities; projects can be found in the entire enterprise in the form of marketing, organization, IT, controlling or other projects [IPMI02, p. 20; DeDi04, p. 12; Gare04, p. 1]. Since large enterprises very often run dozens or even hundreds of parallel projects, management systems for the standardized planning, controlling and coordination of projects are required to ensure efficient and effective project work [Cook02, p. 188]. Such systems guarantee that scarce resources are assigned to those projects that have the highest impact on the realization of the business strategy and that they receive the management attention needed to complete them successfully [BoVö97, p. 17f.; PaRa98, p. 454].

Information systems serve as a basis for such management systems by delivering all necessary information on time and in the required quality [Lech04, p. 16; CIIr02, p. 349-355]. Project information systems develop their full economic potential when they are used to support standardized project management processes and hence supply all relevant stakeholders with the information required to plan, control and coordinate projects. This requires corresponding standards for the production, processing and delivery of project information on the one side and adequate software support on the other. Both tasks – the development of project management standards and the procurement or development of corresponding software systems – are time-consuming and require advanced experience in the field of (multi-)project management, organizational engineering and information technology. It is obvious that reference information models can help to speed up the development of project information systems and that they minimize the risk of project failure. If the reference model applied reflects established and proven business processes, they can also lead to a higher process quality [Schü98, pp. 75ff.].

Up to now the research on project information systems has concentrated on (1) the evaluation of commercially available software applications (e. g. [DwHa92; RaFi94; KoHe95; Ahle03]), (2) the design and prototyping of software applications (e. g. [Kurb94; ScMS96; Ehle97; FrRK97; Stum98; KoHa98; JaMa98; ArGh98]), (3) theoretical considerations regarding the assessment, selection and use of software applications for project management (e. g. [Nick85; Haye93; AhFD00]), and (4) the design and assessment of algorithms mainly for scheduling, resource planning and portfolio management (operations research; e. g. [DoPP00; ChCZ01; Hart02]). Only one research endeavor has focused on recommendations for the design of project information systems in the form of a reference information model [Schl00]. The corresponding research results have not yet been evaluated and concentrate on single-project management only. Hence it can be stated that a thorough research on reference information models for project information systems (in the sense of project program and project portfolio management) is yet to be forthcoming.

Thus, the objective of the research presented in this paper is to develop semi-formal, conceptual reference information models for the enterprise-wide planning, controlling and coordination of projects in matrix project organizations, which can serve as a basis for information system development. They are modeled on a medium level of abstraction to allow their application in various fields, e. g. process management, quality management, workflow management or definition of software requirements. The research is restricted to matrix project organizations, because they can be regarded as the predominant project organization in practice [Rick95, pp. 50-53; Lech97, p. 162].

This paper is structured as follows: Section 2 contains a brief description of the research design and the underlying methodological and theoretical assumptions. Section 3 contains the terminological and conceptual grounding of this paper. Particularly the terms "project controlling" and "reference information model" are discussed. Section 4 presents the so-called M-Model, a conceptual information system architecture which serves as a frame of reference for reference modeling. It embraces all tasks related to the initiation, planning, execution, and termination of projects and explains the management levels involved. Section 5 gives an overview of the reference model and contains selected process and data models created throughout the research process. Section 6 summarizes the results and draws conclusions.

## 2   Research Design

To a large extent, today's reference modeling techniques and methods show a disregard for empirical inquiries as the basis of reference modeling. The authors of the well-established process models for reference modeling indeed refer to the necessity to integrate potential reference model users and domain experts into the construction process. How this integration needs to be done, however, is typically left unanswered [FeLo04a, p. 20]. Moreover, the construction process is normally not documented in reference modeling projects. It does not become clear how the modeler arrives at his models. Very often, the empirical evidence for the reference model construction are not properly recorded [FeLo04b, p. 8].

A comprehensive review of existing models with a description of their core characteristics has been done by FETTKE and LOOS. The corresponding catalogue contains 33 models which were released in the period from 1998 to 2003 in German-speaking countries. Only four of these models explicitly outline the procedure of model construction used. The remaining 29 models contain no or only very vague statements about the construction process. This lack of documentation and empirical evidence makes it difficult to verify the research results. Furthermore, the discourse on the research results and the incremental refinement and improvement of reference models is unnecessarily complicated.

For this reason, in this work special emphasis was put on the empirical foundation of the reference model construction process and its proper documentation. The research design contains detailed information on how potential model users and domain experts are integrated into the construction process and how the construction results are documented so that a higher degree of intelligibility and verifiability is achieved.

The reference modeling is done within a research process that consists of four phases and which has been derived from a process model by Schütte [Schü98, pp. 177ff.]. It has been extended with respect to empirical inquiries and documentation activities. The process consists of the following phases (cf. Figure 1):

- (1) *Problem definition.* In this compulsory first step the research objective is defined and the problem domain is specified as it is documented in the first section of this paper [Schü98, pp. 189ff.; Schl00, p. 79].
- (2) *Exploration and generation of hypotheses.* This second phase consists of three different activities.
  - o (2a) *Construction of a frame of reference.* Here, a conceptual information system architecture is developed which serves as a frame of reference for the following model construction [Schü98, pp. 207ff.; Schl00, p. 79]. This information system architecture is called the M-Model, and is documented in section 4. The M-Model is a result of an extensive examination of existing research results and an analysis of project management case studies documented in the literature. Its structure reflects a widely accepted perspective on project management in general [Alte91; VaBu99].
  - o (2b) *Analysis of project management software systems.* Here, a comprehensive analysis of 28 commercial project management software applications was used to generate hypotheses regarding project management processes, organizational and data structures.
  - o (2c) *Literature review / analysis of PM standards.* Further research carried out by other authors and project management institutions, e. g. about critical success factors in project management or project management organization, is also taken into consideration (e. g. [Lech97; Cook02; PMI04]). (2c) *Construction / refinement of the reference model.* The initial construction of the reference model is based on the knowledge captured from the analysis of project management software systems and the literature review. The reference model can be regarded as a hypothetical construction which does not claim to have universal validity at this point in time. The diagrams contained in the reference model are closely linked to the M-Model, as outlined above.
- (3) *Validation.* The objective of this phase is to validate, refine and stabilize the initial reference model construction.
  - o (3a) *Interviews with domain experts.* A series of interviews with experts in the field of project management and project information sys-

tems was conducted with the objective of gaining further empirical evidence for the reference models and of validating it. This formative evaluation was done in the form of guided interviews [Patt02, p. 227], basically consisting of two parts. In the first part, the knowledge and experience of the domain experts is captured. In the second part, the experts are confronted with the reference model and are asked for detailed feedback regarding the strengths and weaknesses of the model. Furthermore, possible improvements are discussed. In consequence, the reference model is refined or even reconstructed if the interview results render this necessary (return to step 2c). Subsequently, the next interview is conducted. Following an approach by Lincoln & Guba [LiGu85, pp. 234f.], this cyclic process is terminated if insights gained from preceding interview discussions , diminish. On the occurrence of this situation, the conclusion is drawn that consent has been reached among domain experts regarding the reference model's propositions. The selection of domain experts follows both the chain sampling and the theoretical sampling approaches [Patt02, pp. 237-239]. Whereas the domain experts are identified using chain sampling, the interview subject is determined using the frame of reference and theoretical sampling (not all aspects of enterprise-wide project management can be discussed in a single interview).

o (3b) *Practical application*. The validation of the reference model is not only brought about by interviews with domain experts. The reference model has also been validated in the form of application projects. For instance, the model was used to design a project initiation process for a Swiss company. It is also the starting point for the development of a German DIN standard for the exchange of project management data.

o (3c) *Refinement of the reference model*. The experience gained in these projects is also used to refine the reference model.

- (4) *Documentation*. The documentation of the reference model contains the following: (a) *Description of construction process*: The construction process is thoroughly documented, as is indicated here. (b) *Annotations of model elements*: Each model element represented by means of the chosen modeling language is clarified with annotations that include theoretical and empirical references. (c) *Documentation of interview results*: The interview results are made available in the appendix of the documentation so that references to interviews are easily viewable. (d) *Table of model elements*: The appendix contains a table of all reference model elements, e. g. functions, organizational units and data elements.

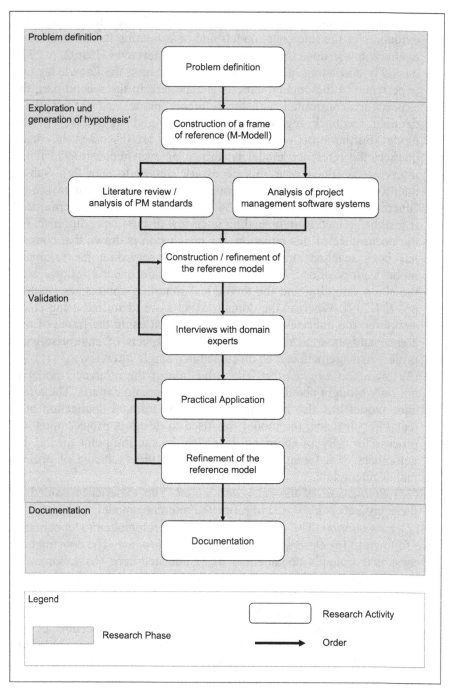

**Figure 1:** The research design

# 3    Terminological and Conceptual Foundation

## 3.1   Project Planning, Controlling and Coordination

According to the German DIN standard, a *project* is defined as an endeavor that is basically characterized by specific circumstances like (1) a defined objective, (2) temporal, financial, personal or other restrictions, (3) a differentiation from other endeavors, and (4) project-specific organization [DIN87].

*Planning* is understood both in the sense of preparing actions and in the sense of preparing decisions. Planning means anticipation of future events in order to collect information needed to make decisions or to perform actions. Planning is typically a systematic process of applying specific methods and tools, very often combined with the definition of objectives, corresponding measures and necessary resources which help to improve a present situation. Planning implies processing information [Horv02, pp. 170ff.].

*Controlling* has to be seen in conjunction with planning. Controlling comprises all forms of monitoring and examination. Controlling has four purposes: (a) It allows the initiating of corrective measures when goals are not reached. (b) It enables learning by comparing the planned and the actual situation. (c) It forms the basis of an assessment of staff performance. (d) And it serves as a preventive measure, since the simple fact that controlling takes place leads to the higher motivation of staff [Horv02, pp. 175ff.].

The need for coordination is a consequence of interdependencies between tasks assigned to different staff. *Coordination* is the reconcilement of single tasks in view of a superior objective. There are several means available to reduce or deal with the need for coordination. The definition of standards is one of those possible solutions. Standards reduce the need for coordination to a management of exceptions. In the context of project management, standardized process and information structures play an important role in the coordination of projects [Adam69, p. 618; Schu99, pp. 203ff.; KiKu92, pp. 102ff.].

## 3.2   Reference Information Models

In recent years, reference information models have become quite popular in the research and development of practical information systems. They have proved to be a suitable means for the specification and implementation of business software as well as for the development and improvement of organizational processes and structures [BeSc96, pp. 27f.].

According to SCHÜTTE, a reference information model is defined as a construction created by a modeler who declares universal elements and relationships of a system as a recommendation so that a centre of reference is created. In this context, reference models are used for the design of information systems, and are typically documented using semi-formal or formal languages [Schü98, p. 69].

Reference information models have a partial universal validity. They are a recommendation on how an information system needs to be designed. The universal validity of a reference information model cannot ultimately be proven [Schü98, p. 70].

## 4    A Frame of Reference: The M-Model

The so-called M-Model is a conceptual software architecture which embraces all tasks related to the initiation, planning, execution, and termination of projects (cf. Figure 2).

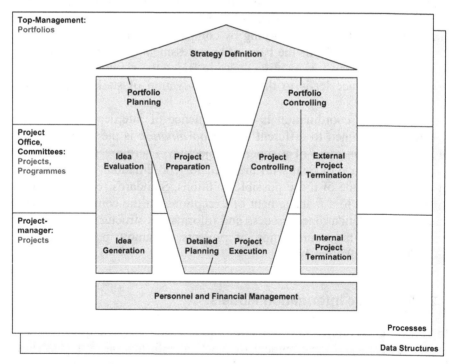

**Figure 2:** The M-Model

It describes the process of enterprise-wide project management (project lifecycle) and explains the management levels involved. The M-Model is used as a frame of reference for the reference model discussed here.

## 4.1 Project Life Cycle

Independent of their individual objectives, projects run through a series of phases which form the project life cycle. At a high level of abstraction, this life cycle can be divided into the following phases [Morr83, pp. 6ff.]:

- *Initiation*: In the initiation phase, project ideas are generated, collected, captured, and examined (*Idea Generation*). Their feasibility, profitability and strategic impact are analyzed so that a final decision about their implementation can be made (*Idea Evaluation*). This phase ends with a formal go/no-go decision made by the management (*Portfolio Planning*).
- *Planning*: In this phase, the project idea is refined into a project plan and the necessary resources (financial, human and other resources) are provided. This phase is similar to the previous one, only it is more detailed. Since the final decision about the project has already been made, the scheduling can be fixed, resource assignments can be made, the budget can be made available, and contracts with external suppliers can be arranged (*Project Preparation*). Additionally, the project plan is refined by the project manager (*Detailed Planning*).
- *Execution*: This phase embraces the realization of the project idea using the resources assigned to the project. It is highly mechanistic; in its ideal form it only consists of an efficient implementation of the project plan prepared in previous phases. The execution of a project frequently leads to a vast expansion of the organization (*Project Execution*). Information about the project execution is collected and analyzed for the purpose of controlling (*Project Controlling*). Information is aggregated to obtain a high-level view of the project situation (*Portfolio Controlling*).
- *Termination*: In the termination phase the project results are installed and submitted to the project sponsor (*Internal Project Termination*). In addition, the enterprise closes the project and endeavors to learn from the experiences made (*External Project Termination*).

These phases are reflected in the shanks of the "M" and are further sub-divided into process steps, as indicated. It is not obligatory for all projects to run through all process steps. Even when a project has finished a complete phase it can still be reasonable to immediately terminate it due to its lack of profitability and feasibility, or its strategic positioning [MeMa95, p. 202].

## 4.2 Management Levels

Three different management levels can be distinguished within the M-Model [Morr83, pp. 8ff.]:

- *Project Manager*: At the level of operational project management, the project manager is responsible for the planning and execution of a single project. This level is represented by the lower third of the M-Model.
- *Project Office/Committees*: The project office is established above the project level. Its primary planning object is the project program, a set of interrelated projects at the departmental level, or any similar organizational unit at the middle level. Typically, the grouping of projects to programs is done by their functional reference (e. g. all IT projects) or their overall objective (e. g. all projects affecting the launch of a new product) [PaRa98, p. 404]. The project office is responsible for the coordination of such a project program. It assigns resources to projects, collects control data and reports to the upper management levels. In addition, it assists project managers and assures that project management standards are adhered to [Burg00, pp. 105f.]. The project office is represented by the middle third of the M-Model. Committees are temporal organizational units that are used to link the primary organization to the project organization. In this case, they typically consist of the most important stakeholders in a project (e. g. the project sponsor, the project manager, line managers, etc.). They are the superior unit for the project manager and have the authority to decide on the process of the project. For instance, the steering committee defines guidelines for the project manager in the form of milestones, priorities, decisions to be made or crucial deadlines. In contrast to the project office, which has a more administrative function, the steering committee has the power to direct and control the project.
- *Top Management*: The management board is represented by the upper third of the M-Model. Since higher management levels do not have the time to coordinate each individual project or program, all projects and programs of larger organizational units, or even the entire enterprise, are combined into a portfolio to increase the clarity of the project landscape and to reduce complexity. The management board is responsible for planning and controlling the portfolio. Its task is to harmonize the business strategy and the project portfolio or, in other words, to derive a

project portfolio from the strategic objectives of the business unit. In doing so, the management board has to take financial and other resource constraints into account. Very often, the management board is assisted by the project office or a similar administrative department. The project office then plans and controls the process of portfolio management and prepares corresponding decision papers.

The strategy definition ("roof" of the "M") is a necessary input for portfolio planning, since it requires a clearly defined business strategy. On the other side, personnel and the financial system (foundation of the "M") are important building blocks since they deliver information necessary for planning and controlling purposes, e. g. staff availability or financial postings.

# 5   Selected Excerpts of the Reference Model

## 5.1   Overview

The reference model consists of 10 basic activity diagrams that correspond to the project lifecycle phases outlined in the scope of the M-Model. Each of these activity diagrams has an assigned class diagram that describes the data structures necessary to run the process. Some activity diagrams are further refined in more detailed process descriptions. In addition to this, the reference model contains class diagrams to specify the interfaces to personnel and financial systems as well as to strategic planning. These diagrams reveal what data is needed from those related systems. Furthermore, some of the fundamental data structures that are used throughout the project lifecycle are also presented in separate class diagrams. This especially concerns organizational structures, basic resource data and elemental classes describing initiatives. Altogether, the reference model comprises 17 activity diagrams, 25 class diagrams, 101 classes, 112 methods and 245 attributes. The level of detail is adequate for organizational modeling and requires further refinement for the purpose of software design and implementation.

In the following, one activity and one class diagram of medium complexity are shown in order to provide an impression of the reference model. The diagrams illustrate the idea generation, which is the first process step in the M-Model. Not all classes are displayed in the class diagram with their attributes and methods. This is because they are discussed and presented in detail in other diagrams of the reference model.

## 5.2   Example: The Idea Generation Process

In the reference model, the idea generation process is covered by the activity *GenerateIdea* (cf. Figure 3). The process starts with staff members collecting and capturing project ideas (action *CreateProjectIdea*). As a result, one or more instances of the class Initiative are created. The capturing of project ideas is ideally the result of a structured idea collection and creativity processes. The newly generated ideas are then checked by the project office (action *CheckProjectIdea*) in order to ascertain whether they meet general requirements, e. g. if they are meaningful and meant seriously or if they are in line with the enterprise's general strategic orientation. Project ideas that are obviously not of any use are already rejected at this early stage. It is also possible for the idea to be regarded as promising, but unsuitable for implementation as a project. In this case, the idea is handed over to the responsible organizational unit. In either case, the status of the project idea is recorded by creating a corresponding instance of the class *InitiativeLifeCyclePhase*.

In order to allow the efficient processing of project ideas, they are classified so that they can easily be found and analyzed (action *ClassifyProjectIdea*). In the course of this classification, the project idea is assigned to one or more classification criteria. With the help of this classification, it is checked whether the project idea already exists, e. g. in the form of a project proposal or even a project in execution (action *CheckExistenceOfProjectIdea*). Such cases are especially common in large organizations. If the project idea already exists, it is deleted. Otherwise it is submitted to the so-called (project) initiation committee (class *InitiationCommittee*). This is recorded by the assignment of a new *InitiativeLifeCyclePhase*.

The initiation committee assesses all project ideas that have been collected since its last meeting (action *AssessProjectIdea*). Assessment is carried out using checklists or scoring models, and can be regarded as a first detailed screening of the project ideas. Typical criteria are, e. g. general strategic conformance or feasibility. Whereas the project office only checks the seriousness of ideas, the initiation committee has to decide whether the preparation of a feasibility study/a business case is promising. The work of the initiation committee leads to a so-called *Assessment*.

The assessment is then used to reach a final decision with regard to the further implementation of the project idea (action *DecideOnProjectIdea*). Three alternative outcomes can be distinguished: (1) The idea is refused. In this case the decision is documented by creating a specific *InitiativeLifeCyclePhase*. (2) The development of a business case is required. Again, a corresponding *InitiativeLifeCyclePhase* is created.

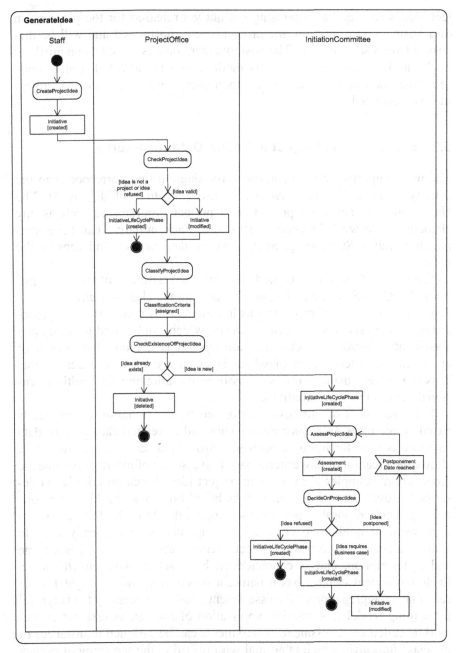

**Figure 3:** The process of generating project ideas (activity *GenerateIdea*)

The process continues in another activity diagram of the reference model, as indicated in the frame of reference (activity *EvaluateIdea*). (3) The project idea is regarded as promising but not yet released for the preparation of a business case. Instead, the project idea is postponed and will be discussed later a second time. The postponement date is stored as an attribute of the initiative, which is why its modification is indicated (object node *Initiative [modified]*). Once the postponement date is reached the project idea is reassessed.

## 5.3   Example: The Project Initiation Data Structures

The most important element in the class diagram that corresponds to the activity diagram *EvaluateIdea* is the class *Initiative* (cf. Figure 4). The class *Initiative* represents projects and project programs as well as any element of the work breakdown structure. Each initiative can have staff members (class *Staff*) assigned that act as idea creators and capture the idea.

The status of initiatives is modeled with the assistance of the Class *InitiativeLifeCyclePhase*, which is associated with the class *Initiative*.

The classification of project ideas is expressed by a corresponding association to the class *ClassificationCriteria*, which can be used to set up any classification system. A classification system is a hierarchic system of classification criteria, each of which is given a name and a description. This is modeled using a reflexive association, allowing for multi-dimensional perspectives on initiatives.

The assessment of initiatives performed by the initiation committee is based on the class *AssessmentFramework* and its related classes. This data structure is used for multiple purposes throughout the reference model. It allows the creation of any criteria-based assessment of information objects. Application examples are screening project ideas based on criteria (as described above), assessing project risks based on a risk checklist or prioritizing project proposals based on a scoring model. In each of these cases, a framework of qualitative criteria is set up that is subsequently used to analyze a specific information object. Hence, each framework has a name and a description, and is characterized by a set of *AssessmentCriteria*. Each assessment criteria has a name, a description and a weight for the case that an aggregation of the assessment results is necessary (as is typical for scoring models). A specific application of such an assessment framework is called an *Assessment*. Assessments can be assigned to instances of the class *Initiative*, which is normal with regard to the screening of project ideas. Each assessment is characterized by a creation date, a summary of the results, a decision made based on the assessment, and a comment.

Detailed, criteria-specific assessment results are stored using the class *As-sessmentResult*. This class is associated with the class *AssessmentCriteria*, has an attribute Result and also allows comments to be captured. Assessments are carried out by staff members; the corresponding association is used to represent this information. Since different assessment frameworks might be necessary for different types of project ideas, there is an association to the class *ClassificationCriteria* in order to show which assessment framework is appropriate for which type of project idea.

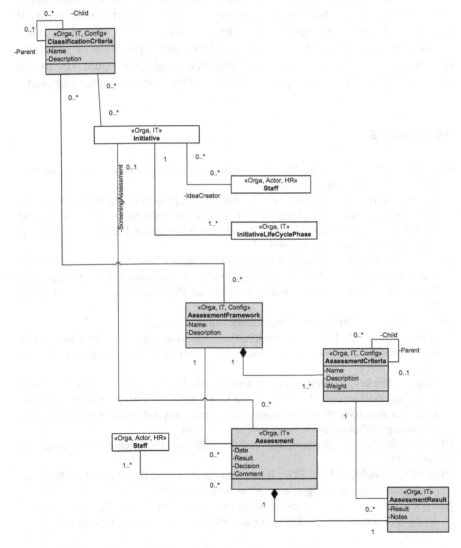

**Figure 4:** Class diagram for the generation of project ideas

## 6    Summary and Conclusion

The reference modeling project presented in this paper took approximately 1½ man-years to achieve. The research process was designed to make both the knowledge of domain experts and software manufacturers available for the model construction. The results can be used directly for organizational projects and the design of project management software.

Currently, the reference model is restricted to matrix project organizations that have some specific characteristics like resource pools and a strong influence of the line management on the project government. It would be desirable to extend the reference model with regard to other forms of project organization. In this context, the application of construction techniques for configurative reference modeling could be useful [BDKK02]. A corresponding research project has currently been initiated.

## References

[Adam69] Adam, D.: Koordinationsprobleme bei dezentralen Entscheidungen. ZfB 39 (1969) 10, pp. 615-632.

[AhFD00] Ahmed, S. M.; Fai, L. K.; De Saram, D.: Project Management Software Selection Criteria in the Hong Kong Construction Industry. In: Proceedings of the International Conference on Construction Information Technology, INCITE 2000. Hong Kong 2000, pp. 604-615

[Ahle03] Ahlemann, F.: Project Management Systems: Typology, State-of-the-Art and Forecast. In: SOVNET, Russian Project Management Association (ed.): Proceedings of the 17th World Congress on Project Management. Moscow 2003.

[Alte91] Alter, R.: Integriertes Projektcontrolling. Gießen 1991.

[ArGh98] Archer, N. P.; Ghasemzadeh, F.: A decision support system for project portfolio selection. International Journal of Technology Management 16 (1998) 1-3, pp. 105-114.

[BDKK02] Becker, J.; Delfmann, P.; Knackstedt, R.; Kuropka, D.: Konfigurative Referenzmodellierung. In: Becker, J., Knackstedt, R. (eds.): Wissensmanagement mit Referenzmodellen. Konzepte für die Anwendungssystem- und Organisationsgestaltung. Heidelberg 2002, pp. 25-144.

[BeSc96] Becker, J.; Schütte, R.: Handelsinformationssysteme. Landsberg am Lech 1996.

[BoVö97] Boutellier, R.; Völker, R.: Erfolg durch innovative Produkte – Bausteine des Innovationsmanagements. München, Wien 1997.

[Burg00] Burghardt, M.: Projektmanagement: Leitfaden für die Planung, Überwachung und Steuerung von Entwicklungsprojekten. 5th edition, Erlangen 2000.

[ChCZ01] Chang, C. K.; Christensen, M. J.; Zhang, T.: Genetic Algorithms for Project Management. In: Annals of Software Engineering Vol. 11. Kluwer Academic Publishers 2001, pp. 107-139.

[ClIr02] Cleland, D. I.; Ireland, L. R.: Project Management – Strategic Design and Implementation. 4th edition, New York et al. 2002.

[Cook02] Cooke-Davies, T.: The "real" success factors on projects. International Journal of Project Management 20 (2002) 3, pp. 185-190.

[DeDi04] Detecon & Diebold Consultants (eds.): Projektmanagement – Ergebnisse einer Umfrage zum Projektmanagement in deutschen Unternehmen. Bonn, Eschborn 2004.

[DIN87] Deutsches Institut für Normung e.V. (ed.): DIN 69901 Begriffe der Projektwirtschaft. Beuth, Berlin 1987.

[DoPP00] Dorndorf, U.; Pesch, E.; Phan-Huy, T.: A Time-Oriented Branch-and-Bound Algorithm for Resource-Constrained Project Scheduling with Generalised Precedence Constraints. Management Science 46 (2000) 10, pp. 1365-1384.

[DwHa92] Dworatschek, S.; Hayek, A.; Marktspiegel Projekt-Management Software – Kriterienkatalog und Leistungsprofile. 3rd edition, Cologne 1992.

[Ehle97] Ehlers, P.: Integriertes Projekt- und Prozeßmanagement auf Basis innovativer Informations- und Kommunikationstechnologien: Das GroupProject-System. Aachen 1997.

[FeLo04a] Fettke, P.; Loos, P.: Referenzmodellierungsforschung. Langfassung eines Aufsatzes. Universität Mainz, ISYM - Information Systems & Management. Mainz 2004.

[FeLo04b] Fettke, P.; Loos, P.: Systematische Erhebung von Referenzmodellen. Ergebnisse der Voruntersuchung. Universität Mainz, ISYM - Information Systems & Management, Mainz 2004.

[FrRK97] Froese, T.; Rankin, J.; Kevin, Y.: Project Management Application Models And Computer And Computer-Assisted Construction Planning in Total Project Systems. International Journal of Construction Information Technology. Special Issues on Integrated Environments 5 (1997) 1, pp. 39-62.

[Gare04] Gareis, R.: Management by projects. In: Schelle, H.; Reschke, H.; Schnopp, R.; Schub, A. (eds.): Projekte erfolgreich managen. 22nd edition, Cologne 2004.

[Gesc93] Geschka, H.: Wettbewerbsfaktor Zeit. Landsberg am Lech 1993.

[Hart02] Hartmann, S.: A Self-Adapting Genetic Algorithm for Project Scheduling under Resource Constraints. Naval Research Logistics 49 (2002), pp. 433-448.

[Haye93] Hayek, A.: Projektmanagement-Software: Anforderungen und Leistungsprofile, Verfahren der Bewertung und Auswahl sowie Nutzungsorganisation von Projekt-Software. Cologne 1993.

[Horv02] Horváth, P.: Controlling. 8th edition, Munich 2002.

[IPMI02] IPMI Universität Bremen, Volkswagen Coaching GmbH (eds.): Project management in Germany – State and Trends. Wolfsburg 2002.

[JaMa98] Jaafari, A.; Manivong, K.: Towards a smart project management information system. International Journal of Project Management 16 (1998) 4, pp. 249-265.

[KiKu92] Kieser, A.; Kubicek, H.: Organisation. 3$^{rd}$ edition, Berlin, New York 1992.

[KoHa98] Komiya, S.; Hazeyama, A.: A Meta-Model of Work Structure of Software project and a Framework for Software Project Management Systems. IEICE Transactions 81 (1998) 12, pp. 1415-1428.

[KoHe95] Kolisch, R.; Hempel, K.: Experimentelle Evaluation der methodischen Fundierung von Projektmanagementsoftware. Bericht Nummer 372. Institut für Betriebswirtschaftslehre, Lehrstuhl für Produktion und Logistik. Universität Kiel 1995.

[Kurb94] Kurbel, K.: Groupware extension for a software-project management system. Internationl Journal of Project Management 12 (1994) 4, pp. 222-229.

[Lech04] Lechler, T.: Erfolgsfaktoren des Projektmanagements – Handlungsempfehlungen aus 448 deutschen Projekten. In: Schelle, H.; Reschke, H.; Schnopp, R.; Schub, A. (eds.): Projekte erfolgreich managen. 22$^{nd}$ edition, Cologne 2004.

[Lech97] Lechler, T.: Erfolgsfaktoren des Projektmanagements. Frankfurt am Main et al. 1997.

[LiGu85] Lincoln, Y. S.; Guba, E. G.: Naturalistic Inquiry. Beverly Hills 1985.

[MeMa95] Meredith, J. R.; Mantel, S. J.: Project Management – A Managerial Approach. 3$^{rd}$ edition. New York et al. 1995.

[Morr83] Morris, P. W. G.: Managing Project Interfaces – Key Points for Project Success. In: Cleland, D. I.; King, W. R. (eds.): Project Management Handbook. New York et al. 1983.

[Nick85] Nickel, E.: Computergestützte Projektinformationssysteme: Grundlagen einer anwendungsbezogenen Gestaltung mit besonderer Berücksichtigung des Großanlagenbaus. Idstein 1985.

[PaRa98] Patzak, G.; Rattay, G.: Projektmanagement – Leitfaden zum Management von Projekten, Projektportfolios und Projektorientierten Unternehmen. 3$^{rd}$ edition, Vienna 1998.

[Patt02] Patton, M. Q.: Qualitative Research & Evaluation Methods. 3$^{rd}$ edition. Thousand Oaks 2002.

[Peri93] Perich, R.: Unternehmensdynamik. Zur Entwicklungsfähigkeit von Organisationen aus zeitlich-dynamischer Sicht. 2$^{nd}$ edition, Bern et al. 1993.

[PMI04] Project Management Institute (ed.): A Guide to the Project Management Body of Knowledge. 3$^{rd}$ edition, Philadelphia 2004.

[RaFi94] Rabl, W.; Fiedler, S.: Projektmanagement-Software: Marktübersicht und Entwicklungstrends. In: Gareis, R. (ed.): Projekte & EDV. Wien 1994, pp. 37-54.

[Rick95] Rickert, D.: Multiprojektmanagement in der industriellen Forschung und Entwicklung. Wiesbaden 1995.

[Sche04] Schelle, H.: Die Lehre vom Projektmanagement: Entwicklung und Stand. In: Schelle, H.; Reschke, H.; Schnopp, R.; Schub, A. (eds.): Projekte erfolgreich managen. 22$^{nd}$ edition, Cologne 2004.

[Schl00] Schlagheck, B.: Objektorientierte Referenzmodelle für das Prozeß- und Projektcontrolling: Grundlagen, Konstruktion, Anwendungsmöglichkeiten. Wiesbaden 2000.

[Schü98] Schütte, R.: Grundsätze ordnungsmäßiger Referenzmodellierung, Konstruktion konfigurations- und anpassungsorientierter Modelle. Wiesbaden 1998.

[Schu99] Schulte-Zurhausen, M.: Organisation. 2$^{nd}$ edition. Munich 1999.

[ScMS96] Schulz, R.; Malzahn, U.; von Schoultz, F.: An Integrated Project Management Information System. Leipzig 1996.

[Stum98] Stummer, C.: Projektauswahl im betrieblichen F&E-Management. Ein interaktives Entscheidungsunterstützungssystem. Wiesbaden 1998.

[Turn99] Turner, J. R.: The handbook of project-based management. London et al. 1999.

[VaBu99] Vahs, D.; Burmester, R.: Innovationsmanagement: Von der Produktidee zur erfolgreichen Vermarktung. Stuttgart 1999.

# Application-Oriented Evaluation of the SDM Reference Model: Framework, Instantiation and Initial Findings

Tilo Böhmann, Michael Schermann, Helmut Krcmar

**Abstract:** *Reference models have become fundamental tools in Information Systems research owing to the associated claim of reusing existing knowledge and getting faster and better solutions by adapting reference models instead of modeling and developing them individually. While the advantages are widely stated they are currently not reflected in documented acceptance and usage of reference models in practice. This calls for empirical substantiation of the claims of reference models. This paper summarizes a framework for the application-oriented evaluation of reference models and instantiates the framework for a reference model for Service Data Management (SDM). We argue that the claim of a reference model should be evaluated in three distinct stages of a reference model supply chain: reference modeling, solution design, and business transformation. Based on these stages, we propose a detailed evaluation plan using the Goal-Question-Metric approach and present first evaluation results, which have already led to improvements of the reference model. The paper is intended as stimulus for discussing viable approaches to empirically support research on reference modeling.*

## 1 The Challenge of Reference Model Evaluation

Reference models are considered as important tools in Information Systems research and practical system development alike [FeLo04a]. Evaluating reference models and choosing among the increasing number of alternatives thus becomes a pressing issue for researchers and practitioners alike.

Generally, *reference models* are defined as semantically and pragmatically generalized models [BeSc04]. They are constructed for reuse, e. g. as framework or architecture of application models [LoFe05; RoSc97]. Reference models can therefore be used as a starting point for developing information systems or organizational design [BDKK02]. Designers can refer to reference models when developing application models, implying that reference models provide recommendations for solving application problems. Reference models can thus be seen as blueprints for accelerating problem-solving [BeSc04; MiZh00]. The term *reference model* implies that using reference models may deliver faster solutions, higher quality or lower cost compared to individually constructed solutions by reusing the knowledge embodied in the reference model. From an empirical standpoint, this claim of utility needs to be demonstrated through successful applications of the model [Fran98]. Often, reference models lack proper evaluation and the actual impact and utility remains abstract and vague [FeLo03a]. Evaluation of reference models thus has to substantiate or refute these claims [HMPR04].

Admittedly, it is easier to demand evaluation than to implement it. We argue that evaluation requires a discussion of alternative conceptualizations of the potential value of reference model and their corresponding definitions of the object and objectives of evaluation in order to select realistic goals for evaluation for a given reference model. In recent discussions of reference model evaluation, much emphasis has been put on assessing the quality of the model as such. While certainly intricate and nontrivial, we argue this is just the first step towards a reference model evaluation. Being a primarily analytical exercise, researchers can usually conduct this type of evaluation in the absence of actual application of a reference model. The notion of reference models, however, at least implies benefits of reuse that accrue to the users of reference models. We therefore argue that it is critical to work towards evaluation, which considers the model quality, the user of the reference model, and the user of the result of the reference modeling effort as well.

We understand *evaluation* as the systematic assessment of an object in order to derive an extent of accordance of the evaluation object with certain goals [Fran98; Krom01; Hein02]. An evaluation approach comprises four components: an evaluation object, a set of evaluation objectives, a set of evaluation criteria, a set of evaluation indicators or metrics each of which is highly dependent of the other components [Hein02].

The *evaluation object* is the specific artifact in question as well as its environment [Krom01]. For example in an organization, the motivation or skills of the people determine the usefulness of an innovative application probably more than its technical aspects [HMPR04]. The set of evaluation objectives determine the goals and purpose of the evaluation project in question. The set of *evaluation objectives* is highly dependent on the evaluating subject, for example evaluation is commonly used to prepare or to legitimate decisions [Fran98; Reek00]. In real life settings it is highly improbable that all available aspects of an artifact can be or has to be evaluated. Thus, a certain set of *evaluation criteria* needs to be determined. The selected criteria and the transparency of the process that has been used to deduce criteria largely determine the quality of the evaluation results. Furthermore evaluation criteria may have to reflect different stakeholders of the artifact [Wang00]. Then, evaluation criteria have to be mapped to attributes of the artifact's structure in order to derive *evaluation metrics*, which in turn describe the specific information required to evaluate according to a given criterion [Krom01].

Overall, the claim of reference models is pivotally linked to their application in the design and implementation of solutions for different contexts. Evaluation of reference models should therefore strive to assess the impact of their application to substantiate or refute their claim to utility for designing solutions for a class of problems in a given domain.

In the remainder of this paper, we proceed as follows: first we introduce a reference model for service data management as evaluation object. Thereafter we summarize the reference model supply chain as a systematic framework for the application-oriented evaluation of reference models, that is focusing on evaluation the usage and benefits of reference models (already presented in [BWFK04]). We use the Goal-Question-Metric approach in order to instantiate the evaluation framework. By applying the framework to the SDM reference model we discuss the evaluation plan for the SDM reference model and present some first results. We conclude with a short summary and an outlook to future work.

## 2 The SDM Reference Model

Facing saturated product-oriented markets, the services sector plays an important role for developing potentials to growth. As services become more and more complex and their relevance for economic success becomes evidently, systematic development and delivery of services has become an important challenge to academic research [BuMe01; Fähn98]. Especially the market for services relying on information technology (so called IT services) has changed in recent history. Current industry trends suggest that the evolution of IT services will follow the path of utilities. Not surprisingly, service providers strive to achieve greater productivity through extensive automation of customization, provisioning, and monitoring of IT services. IT service providers thus face a challenge similar to that of industrial enterprises: to establish an integrated management of service data across different stages of the service value chain [Böhm04]. Similar to product data management (PDM), service data management (SDM) enables providers to manage services throughout their lifecycle and across different functions, such as engineering, offering, selling, delivering and controlling services. This integration requires a shared model of IT services that displays the common concepts of divergent representation of services for different functions of service management [FäAu03].

Despite the traditional view on services as distinct from products because of their intangible nature and the integration of customers in service delivery, current developments towards mass-customized IT services increase the similarity to products. Consequently, SDM may leverage established concepts for managing product data. The dynamic nature of the field has lead to a plethora of definitions, concepts, and models of IT services. One key driver of this diversity is the variety of tools used for supporting and automating specific functions of service delivery. The key challenge for SDM is to identify the common concepts used in the approaches applied in this field. The role of service data management is to support the information logistics in both, service engineering and service delivery [BWFK04]. The SDM reference model is supposed to capture necessary data structures for service data management.

In the following, we will shortly introduce the main concepts of the SDM reference model. More in-depth information can be found in [BWFK04; FWBK05]. The main concept of the SDM reference model is the IT service *module*. We argue that the current trends towards industrialization and mass-customization in the IT services sector, can best be coped with, if service offerings are highly customizable, yet standardized in their delivery. [Böhm04] and [Burr00] have therefore proposed the idea of service modularization. IT services are being built by using a service architecture consisting of service modules. A service module provides a coherent set of functionality, e. g. internet connectivity. Based on such an *architecture* it is possible to combine modules in order to create service products. (We are aware of the contradiction in this term. We understand product as a standardized set of functionality, which is offered to a specific market). Such a *service product* is developed based on the perceived requirements of specific markets and defines the attributes and quality aspects of a solution in a consistent way [BWFK04]. Furthermore, service contracts proposals or catalogues are based on products and their specification of functionality. In case a client purchases a service product is has to be adapted to the client's individual requirements and situation. We call such an adapted service product a *service configuration*. The actual contract between service provider and client refers to the service configuration [BWFK04]. Figure 1 shows the relevant part of the SDM reference model as a UML class diagram [OMG03].

As depicted in Figure 1, the classes *ServiceArchitecture*, *ServiceProduct* and *ServiceConfiguration* are related by associations. A *ServiceProduct* is always associated with one *ServiceArchitecture*. A *ServiceConfiguration* is always associated with a *ServiceProduct*, respectively. A *ServiceArchitecture* consists of different *Modules*. A *Module* is an aggregation of different attributes with corresponding values. The relationship between

*Modules* and the tiers of S*erviceArchitecture*, *ServiceProduct* and *Service-Configuration* is expressed by using association classes. Such a three-tiered conceptualization of IT services allows separating different concerns and requirements, such as service engineering, service marketing, and service delivery. Furthermore, it allows introducing different representations of IT service, for example in case of *ProductModules* as part of a service catalogue. More detailed information about the reference model and its theoretical background may be found in [BWFK04; FWBK05].

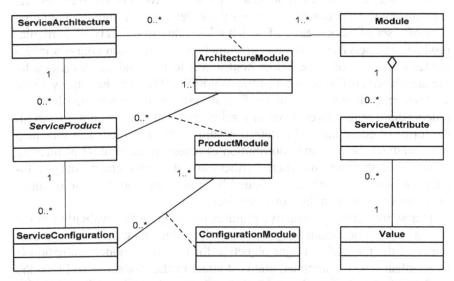

**Figure 1:** Module, Architecture, Product and Configuration in the SDM reference model (based on [BWFK04])

## 3 A Framework for Reference Model Evaluation

In the following we will discuss reference model supply chains as an approach to differentiate evaluation perspectives based on a market-oriented point of view [BöSK07]. Furthermore, we introduce the Goal-Question-Metric approach in order to allow instantiating the reference model supply chain.

### 3.1 The Reference Model Supply Chain

There are various objectives of reference models and numerous possible areas of applications [ScSW02]. Likewise, there is a variety of stakeholders involved in the construction and, especially, in the use of reference models. Consequently, it is often difficult to reach consensus on the objectives of the evaluation of reference models. Less apparent, this seems to be linked to failing to agree on the object of evaluation. In the following section, we argue that we can gain some clarity in identifying the object and matching objectives for the evaluation of reference models by using analogy of supply chain analysis [BöSK07].

The pivotal assumption of a supply chain perspective is the focus on the end customer and his or her demand [WoJR90]. Products and services create value to the customer by meeting these demands. A supply chain consists of a set of actors, each of which adds value to delivery of particular products and services to the end customer. A supply chain analysis investigates how each of these actors contributes to the total value created by the supply chain [WoJR90; Fish97; Wild00]. Although the supply chain analysis extends beyond a single firm it assumes the actors involved are independent firms linked through market transactions, i. e. non-hierarchical forms of coordination [Wild00]. A supply chain analysis can thus help to understand the role and contribution of actors in the context of meeting demands of the end customer. Furthermore, a supply chain analysis focuses on increasing the value created by improving coordination of interdependent activities in the supply chain.

This supply chain perspective requires focusing on the evaluation of the utility of reference models by assessing the value created for the end customer of the models. A major objective for reference model evaluation is to establish who the intended end customers of the model are and how the model creates value for them. Secondly, the supply chain analysis helps to identify involved parties, e. g. software development companies and how these parties contribute to creating and delivering reference models. This actor-centric perspective calls for evaluating the contribution of individual actors to the utility of the reference model for the end customer.

## 3.2   The Value of Reference Models: Output and Outcome

The notion of value is pivotal to a supply chain analysis and the evaluation of reference models alike. Yet determining the value of reference model, that is, their contribution to business or organizational performance of the users of reference models is fraught with difficulties. The suggested possible uses of reference models often emphasize that reference models are a means to facilitate a business initiative.

The supply chain perspective effectively treats reference models as products or services whose use is expected to yield benefits to the customer [BrBu04]. The supply chain analogy also emphasizes the distribution of work in delivering a product or service to its end-customers. These stages of a supply chain provide a high-level view of the transformations that are necessary to convert primary inputs into finished goods. Both aspects are relevant to the evaluation of reference models. Reference modeling intends to enable reuse of models [FeLo04a]. This corresponds to different stages of a supply chain because reuse implies a distribution of work between the construction of a reference model and its application. As [LoFe05] emphasize, both processes may be organizational and temporal separated.

As reference models may be seen as tools for problem solving, they are, figuratively speaking, more similar to primary or intermediate goods than to finished goods. For the discussion of reference model evaluation one can therefore treat the construction of a reference model as the origin of a supply chain and identify the succeeding stages that are required to transform the input of a reference model into something valuable to a particular end-customer.

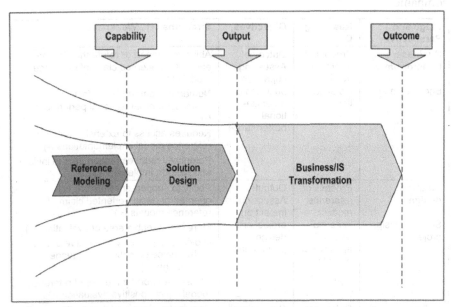

**Figure 2:** The reference model supply chain: Stages and evaluation objectives

Assessing the value of reference models from a supply chain perspective calls for an evaluation of ideally the outcomes of the application of reference models, or at least the output of their application. A similar line of reasoning is well established within evaluation research that differentiates output from outcomes of a particular measure [Krom01; Love04]. Outputs are directly observable results of a measure, while outcomes assess the effects of producing the outputs on the environments into which they are released.

Therefore one can conceptualize a simple reference model supply chain with three stages (cf. Figure 2): reference modeling, solution design, and business or IS transformation. Outcomes and outputs directly correspond to stages of this supply chain. Business or IS transformation yields outcomes of the application of reference models, as this stage reflects the impacts of changing information systems or business practices with the help of reference models. The reference model essentially captures a blueprint for a business solution. The impact results from implementing this solution in a particular organization. The end-customer of the supply chain is thus the owner of the implementation of a solution, e. g. a manager responsible for the performance of a business unit or IS unit in which the solution is implemented. Based on these basic stages the reference model supply chain may be extended by introducing intermediary phases, i. e. consulting companies.

| Stage and Perspective | Resulting Object | Objectives | Strengths (+) / Weaknesses (-) |
|---|---|---|---|
| **Business transformation**<br><br>End customer | Product of reference model instantiation | Outcome: Assessing impact on business or organizational performance | Ability to support or refute the strongest application-oriented claim of reference model (+)<br>Numerous confounding effects on business or organizational performance (-)<br>Requires access to extensive data on reference model implementations (-)<br>Potentially requires researchers to initiate and support implementations (-) |
| **Solution design**<br><br>Solution design project | Process of reference model instantiation and application models | Output: Assessing impact on project or design performance | Ability to support or refute project-oriented or design-oriented claim of reference models (+)<br>More manageable area of evaluation (+)<br>Provides opportunity to observe effects of the choice of modeling language or tool support (+)<br>Weaker support for the use of reference models given positive evaluation (-) |
| **Reference modeling**<br><br>Reference model constructor | Reference model | Capabilities: Assessing model quality or construction performance | Does not require model instantiation (+)<br>No evaluation of reference model application (-) |

**Table 1:** Objects and objectives of evaluation in the reference model supply chain (according to [BöSK07])

In sum, taking a supply chain perspective, there are three distinct approaches to perform an evaluation of reference models, each of which is associated with a distinct object of evaluation and different measure of performance of the impact of reference model application (cf. Table 1).

## 3.3  Instantiation of the Framework: the Goal-Question-Metric Approach

As evaluating of IT artifacts, such as models or implementations, is a pressing issue in computer science and information systems research alike, many approaches for evaluating artifacts have been proposed [FeLo03a; HMPR04; HeHä00]. When instantiating the reference model supply chain analogy, we require a multi-perspective approach for determining different aspects of the reference model and the reference modeling process, which allows specifying evaluation objectives based on different perspectives as well as the association of specific evaluation metrics.

To incorporate different perspectives of stakeholders as well as to instantiate objectives into specific measurable attributes of evaluation objects we have chosen the Goal-Question-Metric (GQM) approach, originally developed by NASA and later transferred to the field of information systems, especially to software engineering [Wang00; BaCR02]. GQM provides a general framework for specifying evaluation objectives based on different perspectives as well as deriving measurable attributes of artifacts. GQM aims at systematically providing measurement mechanisms for evaluating IT artifacts. Although primarily used in software engineering projects, we argue that GQM is suitable for evaluating artifacts, processes and resources, which means that all three stages of the reference model supply chain can be covered by GQM [Wang00].

As we have discussed above, the constituents of evaluation efforts are objectives, criteria and metrics. GQM incorporates these constituents as follows: GQM starts with goals, which determine the realm of successful endeavors. Each goal consists of a purpose (why evaluating?), an issue (focusing on what?), an object or process (evaluating what?), and a certain viewpoint reflecting the person or group stating the goal (evaluating for whom?) [Wang00; BaCR02]. This quadruple therefore specifies the evaluation object and the evaluation subject. Furthermore, the specific context (in our case the supply chain stages) of goals has to be considered [Wang00; HoKe97].

In order to establish a form of measurement of the achievement of goals, evaluation criteria are formulated as questions. Answers to these questions are likely containing information necessary for measuring the achievement. In the next step, metrics are developed to provide means for identifying, and defining the necessary quantitative or qualitative data sources, which are needed to answer the questions [BaCR02]. Metrics can provide data for different questions and goals. During the process of evaluation the GQM trees of goals, questions, and metrics is interpreted from bottom-up (cf. Table 2 for an example).

| Goal | Purpose | Improve |
|---|---|---|
| | Issue | cost, time, and quality of |
| | Object/Process | solution design by using the SDM reference model |
| | Viewpoint | from a designer's point of view |
| Question 1 | How has been the usage of the SDM reference model? | |
| | Metric 1 | Number of projects applying the reference model |
| | Metric 2 | Number of successful projects using the reference model |
| | Metric 3 | Cases Studies of successfully accomplished projects using the SDM reference model |

**Table 2:** Example of a goal, question, and metrics

Hence, GQM allows the top-down development of problem-specific means of measuring assumed quality-relevant aspects of the evaluation object. By interpreting the results bottom-up it is ensured, that the rationale of metrics and questions is considered [DiHL96]. Furthermore, it incorporates the ability to state goals and questions based on different perspectives of stakeholders as well as their specific contexts. Applying the GQM approach on the evaluation of reference models allows incorporating different evaluation contexts, different perspectives as well as deriving specific metrics for evaluation.

GQM is supposed to be part of an organizational structure called experience factory [BaCR02]. Within the experience factory a different roles are specified, that are responsible for defining and analyzing goals, questions and metrics in coordination with development teams [BaCR02]. Such an evaluation structure has to be established for evaluating reference models as well.

## 4    Evaluation Plan for the SDM Reference Model

Based on the reference model supply chain and the GQM approach we now present the evaluation plan for the SDM reference model. The reference model supply chain as well as the GQM approach has to be instantiated and adapted for the reference model that is subject to an evaluation. As we have analyzed the object and objectives of an application-oriented reference model evaluation above (cf. table 1), the SDM evaluation framework consists of three main phases of the reference model supply chain: reference modeling, solution design and business transformation.

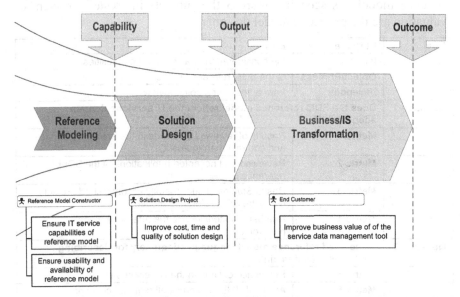

**Figure 3:** Overview of the goals according to the phases of the reference model supply chain

The evaluation phase *reference modeling* focus on the evaluation of the actual quality of the reference model, whereas the phase *solution design* assesses the impact of the reference model in its intended field of application: solution design projects and their output. The phase *business transformation* in turn comprises the evaluation of the outcome – the impact on business or organizational performance. Figure 3 shows the overall process of evaluating the SDM reference model according to the GQM approach.

As depicted in Figure 3, each stage has claims expressed by the goals associated. Furthermore, different stakeholders are interested in the fulfillment of the goals, when using the SDM reference model. In the following, the goals are specified by questions and metrics according to the specific situation of the SDM reference model. We will discuss pivotal questions and metrics.

### Stage 1: Reference Modeling

Table 3 shows the goals of an evaluation derived from the stage of reference modeling. Within the reference modeling stage, evaluation aims firstly at assessing the capabilities of the reference model. Furthermore, the SDM reference model should be usable as well as publicly available. These goals aim at ensuring the basis of a reference character of the SDM reference model. As seen in Figure 3 the subjects interested in such an evaluation are the reference model designers.

| Goal | Purpose | Ensure |
|---|---|---|
| | Issue | the consideration of all required capabilities |
| | Object/Process | of the SDM reference model |
| | Viewpoint | from a designer's point of view |
| Question 1 | Does the SDM reference model reflect the IT services domain adequately? | |
| | Metric 1 | Results of reviews by experts in the area of IT-services and contract management |
| | Metric 2 | Reviewed and accepted publications of the SDM reference model |
| | Metric 3 | Cases Studies of successfully accomplished projects using the SDM reference model |
| | Metric 4 | Number of extensions to the reference model per project |
| Question 2 | Is the used reference model language adequately for describing the IT services domain? | |
| | Metric 5 | Relevance of UML in the IT services industry |
| | Metric 6 | Ability of UML to express all required concepts |
| | Metric 7 | Tool support for UML |
| Goal | Purpose | Ensure |
| | Issue | the usability and availability |
| | Object/Process | of the SDM reference model |
| | Viewpoint | from a designate customer's point of view |
| Question 3 | Is the SDM reference model understandable to potential customers? | |
| | Metric 8 | Time of orientation phase needed in full time equivalents |
| | Metric 9 | Existing trainings for potential customers |
| | Metric 10 | Subjective analysis of the documentation |
| Question 4 | Is the SDM reference model well known in the IT services market? | |
| | Metric 2 | Reviewed and accepted publications of the SDM reference model |
| | Metric 11 | Number of intermediaries of the SDM reference model |
| | Metric 12 | Number of co-development partners for the SDM reference model |

**Table 3:** Goals, questions and metrics for the reference modeling stage

The first goal is about ensuring the completeness of capabilities of the reference model. Question 1 therefore deals with the adequateness of the SDM reference model for the IT services domain. The SDM reference model has to be able to reflect all necessary concepts of the IT services domain. In order to ensure this quality attribute the metrics described in table 2 has been used as data sources. The SDM reference model has been developed in cooperation with experts of the IT services industry, especially in the area of contract management. A metric for the academic quality of the model are peer-reviewed publications. A more detailed metric analysis also account for the reputation or impact of the journals and conferences. Furthermore, the reference model has to be used successfully in contract management projects. Also, the occurrence and frequency of extension made to the SDM reference model in projects indicates whether the SDM reference model reflects the IT services domain adequately.

Question 2 deals with the appropriateness of the used modeling language UML. To answer this question it is necessary to analyze the diffusion of UML among probable customers in the IT services domain. As UML is one of the predominate modeling languages, competence in UML can be fairly assumed for designated customers. Nevertheless, in order to evaluate the fit of the reference model with a certain market segment, UML may not be that ubiquitous after all. Especially for requirements analysis in small and midsized companies, modeling languages like UML could be unsuitable [BDKK02].

The second goal of the reference modeling phase is to ensure the usability of the reference model. In order to assess the usability of the SDM reference model, we especially consider important the availability of documentations as well as trainings. Potential users have to be asked, whether the documentation of the SDM reference model is suitable or not. A second important aspect of this goal is the availability of the reference model in the designated market of the IT services industry. Here again, publications are a suitable metric. Furthermore the number of committed intermediaries and co-developers, such as companies or expert alliances is relevant to the availability and diffusion.

Furthermore, this catalogue of questions can be extended to ensuring the model quality, e. g. by ontological analysis or applying the guidelines of modeling [FeLo03b; ScRo98]. From an application-oriented perspective, such questions have to be dealt with during the reference modeling project.

## Stage 2: Solution Design

During the second stage in the reference model supply chain – solution design – the outputs of applying the reference model are of interest. According to [BeSc04] development and application of reference models is motivated by the prospect of reducing cost, enhancing revenues, or minimizing risks. As we want to evaluate the output of reference modeling, the goal of this stage is improving of cost, time, and quality of the solution design project, which has to be supported by the appliance of the SDM reference model. The perspective of evaluation is the perspective of solution design project.

| Goal | Purpose | Improve |
|---|---|---|
| | Issue | cost, time, and quality of |
| | Object/ Process | solution design by using the SDM reference model |
| | Viewpoint | from a designer's point of view |
| Question 1 | What has been the usage of the SDM reference model? | |
| | Metric 1 | Number of projects applying the reference model |
| | Metric 2 | Number of successful projects using the reference model |
| | Metric 3 | Cases Studies of successfully accomplished projects using the SDM reference model |
| Question 2 | Did the appliance of the SDM reference model affect the speed of solution design? | |
| | Metric 4 | Time needed to conclude the functional requirements analysis for service contract management projects (in full time equivalents) |
| | Metric 5 | Time needed to adapt and extend a SDM reference model and finalize the derived application models |
| | Metric 6 | Change requests of future users of models during the solution design |
| | Metric 7 | Subjective evaluation of acceptance of and satisfaction with the solution design |
| Question 3 | Did the appliance of the SDM reference model affect the costs of the solution design? | |
| | Metric 8 | Costs associated with the solution design |
| | Metric 9 | Relative costs associated with the solution design compared to other phases |
| | Metric 10 | Subjective evaluation of cost effects of the solution design |
| Question 4 | Did the appliance of the SDM reference model affect the quality of the solution design? | |
| | Metric 11 | Change requests before the solution design has been accepted |
| | Metric 12 | Has the SDM reference model been recommended to other project teams |
| | Metric 13 | Willingness of a project team to use the reference model again |

**Table 4:** Goal, questions and metric to evaluate the solution design stage

Naturally, the occurrence and frequency of applying the reference model is a precondition to assess any outputs (question 1). Question 2 to 4 aim at evaluating the output of the reference model according to cost, time, and quality of the results of solution design projects. Take for example metric 4, which measures the amount of time needed to agree on a certain set of functional requirements. Assuming the SDM reference model has a reference character, the amount of full time equivalents should be perceived as significantly lower compared with other projects or experience. Furthermore, the amount of time needed to adapt and extend the reference model should at least be less than the time of individual modeling. The amount and complexity of change request concerning functional aspects of the designed solution could be a suitable output indicator during the solution design.

## Stage 3: Business Transformation

In the stage of business transformation the goal of a reference model should be a positive impact of the implemented solution – in case of the SDM reference model a service management system based on the SDM reference model.

| Goal | Purpose | Improve |
| --- | --- | --- |
| | Issue | business value |
| | Object/Process | of the service data management tool |
| | Viewpoint | from an end customers point of view |
| Question 1 | Has the solution design been implemented? | |
| | Metric 1 | Successful implementation project |
| | Metric 2 | Deployable SDM system |
| Question 2 | Has the solution been accepted by the end customer? | |
| | Metric 3 | Number of active users |
| | Metric 4 | Number of installations |
| Question 3 | What have been the quality drawbacks of contract management before deploying the contract management system? | |
| | Metric 5 | Subjective assessment by service managers |
| | Metric 6 | Failure rate |
| | Metric 7 | Time needed for contract change management |
| | Metric 8 | Time needed for contract negotiation |
| Question 4 | Is the contract management system improving the contract management process? | |
| | Metric 5 | Subjective assessment by service managers |
| | Metric 6 | Failure rate |
| | Metric 7 | Time needed for change management |
| | Metric 8 | Time needed for contract negotiation |
| Question 5 | Does the IT services industry accept the SDM reference model as reference model? | |
| | Metric 9 | End customer involvement in further refinement of the SDM reference model |
| | Metric 10 | Involvement of co-developers and intermediaries in the refinement of the SDM reference model |
| | Metric 11 | Standard software based on the SDM reference model available |

**Table 5:** Goal, questions and metrics for the business transformation stage

As we have discussed above, assessing the business transformation is the most difficult part in evaluating reference models. Therefore, we have firstly compiled questions and metrics which serve as *sine qua non* for any impact on business processes (Question 1 and 2). Furthermore, we are focusing on the main problems usually associated with service management in the IT services industry, the management of service level agreements and service contracts [BöKr05; BöKr04a; BöKr04b]. Question 1 seems trivial but as [FeLo04b] have found, only few reference models have been actually implemented. If implemented, subsequently the acceptance of a service management system by the end customer has to be assessed. Furthermore, comparing the contract management process before (question 3) and after (question 4) the contract management system has been introduced could provide valuable input for assessing the impact of the reference model. We argue that a pivotal key metric for assessing the likelihood of impact of the SDM reference model is the involvement of end customers, intermediaries and co-developers in the further refinement of the SDM reference model.

## 5    First Results

The current development and transfer of the SDM reference models has provided us with first opportunities to implement the evaluation framework. After providing a brief overview of the evaluation and application of the reference model, we discuss first findings of the ongoing implementation of the evaluation framework.

We have developed the SDM reference model in close interaction with experts on service management and IT services both for its initial development (as reported in [BWFK04; FWBK05]) and for its ongoing extension. For the initial version, we could draw on the expertise of service level management specialists of a German IT service provider (among the top 25 of the market). For the current extension (publication pending) a working group with service management experts from a leading enterprise software vendor provided feedback to the model and suggestions for its extension.

Moreover, the reference model has been implemented twice. As a first step, we created a research prototype that allowed us to demonstrate the core concepts of the reference models and their applications [BWFK04; FWBK05]. We used the prototype to conduct usability assessments with experts from the IT service provider based on typical use cases of contract management and the provider's service catalogue. As the second step, a small software company decided to build a commercial SDM application based on the published model. The company won a project with an Application Service Provider (ASP). The provider is about to go live with the SDM application for supporting and automating service engineering, contract management and billing for a multinational customer base.

This background allows us to report first findings of the application-oriented evaluation of the SDM reference model. As the overall application projects and their assessment are ongoing, these findings address only selected parts of the framework.

The goal of the *reference modeling stage* is to assess the capabilities of the reference model. The first criterion for evaluation is the degree to which the SDM reference model reflects the IT services domain adequately. The model quality has benefited from the feedback and input of several experts in the domains of IT services and service management (Metric 1). It also has been published in a peer-reviewed publication (Metric 2). So far, a case study of a project using the reference model is in progress but not yet completed (Metric 3). This extensive feedback has confirmed many parts of the model but also raised two critical issues about the role of modularization and product-orientation (cf. next section). Since the community of direct users of the model is still in its infancy it is too early to provide robust answers to the remainder of the criteria for assessing the model's capabilities (Questions 2-4 of the framework).

The goal for the *solution design stage* is to assess the impact of using the reference model on developing new solutions in the domain of the model. The first criterion is the extent to which the model is applied in solution design projects. The commercial software development project represents one instance where the model is used in designing a service data management solution for an IT service provider. As the software is close to going live, the project may count as a successful project (Metrics 1 and 2). No case studies have been reported yet (Metric 3). Overall, the use of the reference model had a significant effect on the solution design. Of the overall solution design and development project, the software company used only 15% of the total project hours for requirements analysis and conceptual design, thus affecting time and cost of the project. We can assume that time and cost of requirements analysis and conceptual would have been higher without using the SDM reference model (Metric 4, 8 & 9). The reference model did not cover all business requirements initially so that extensions were necessary. The core concepts of the conceptual design, however, remained unchanged throughout design and implementation of the software application. Moreover, the customer of the implementation perceived the reference model as a mark of quality (Metric 7). The reference was thus essential for winning the project for the proposed application. We currently cannot report data on the other metrics.

The goal of the *business transformation stage* is to evaluate the effect of using a solution on business or organizational performance. There is currently no data available on the business impact of using the SDM software on business processes for service engineering, contract management, and billing from the project with the IT service provider. We plan, however, to collect and report these data at a later stage.

While providing summative results regarding the capabilities of the reference model and its impact on solution design, the application and evaluation also rendered formative results for further improvements of the model.

## 6    Limitations

The first results of applying the evaluation framework to the SDM reference model exhibits limitations both of the reference model and the framework.

A *conceptual limitation* of the reference model is the underlying assumption of mass-customized, commodity-type IT services. Accordingly, the SDM model assumes a strong productization of service design and a modular delivery system for these services. Both the review with service management experts and the implementation exposed this assumption as a limitation of the model. The IT service provider that is about to use the SDM software agrees on the desirability of this approach to service engineering and delivery but has not yet fully implemented it. Likewise, service management experts from the workgroup with the enterprise software vendor doubted that for this assumption can hold for all IT service providers using SDM software.

To avoid this limitation, the SDM reference model should be configurable regarding the inclusion or exclusion of service products as a layer between a shared service architecture and customer-specific service configurations. Moreover, the reference model should allow for flexible composition of service delivery elements rather than assuming a non-hierarchical set of service delivery modules.

Furthermore, we are aware that there are *limitations of the proposed implementation of the evaluation framework*. The GQM approach yields only a coarse approximation of the impact of reference model, particularly for the business transformation stage. The evaluation rests on pragmatic indicators for capability, project performance, or business and organization performance. Consequently, the proposed instantiation of the reference model supply-chain does not yet offer a rigorous explanation of the impact of the reference model. A typical variance-based explanation [Mohr82] may be impossible, however, for the business transformation stage. Numerous confounding factors impede with the isolation of the impact of model capabilities on business or organizational performance. More promising approaches may be an approximation of the outcomes of reference models by estimating their market value or using the reference model supply chain as a basis for a process based explanation of impact [Mohr82].

## 7   Conclusion and Outlook

The application-oriented evaluation is a critical challenge for researchers constructing and using reference models. It is necessary to substantiate empirically the advantages commonly associated with reference models. We have proposed one approach for such an evaluation based on the framework of a reference model supply chain. The instantiated supply chain using a Goal-Question-Metric logic and the first findings show how such an approach can be practically applied.

Good design research needs to address the issue of evaluation. The application-oriented evaluation of reference models, however, is still in its infancy. This paper is intended to stimulate the discussion about viable and robust ways of empirical support for reference modeling research. Future work could address two deficits of the current state of the application-oriented evaluation of reference models. First and foremost, more evaluations are required. To enable such evaluations, constructors should be more explicit about the intended use of a reference model and hence their model's claim to utility. Secondly, one could imagine an evaluation maturity model for design research that indicates the extent to which a reference model was subjected to an evaluation regarding its capabilities, its impacts on solution design and effects on business value. Better evaluation should foster construction and use of reference models in a business context.

## References

[BaCR02] Basili, V. R.; Caldiera, G.; Rombach, H. D.: The Goal Question Metric Paradigm. In: Marchiniak J. J. (ed.): Encyclopedia of Software Engineering. New York 2002, pp. 578-583.

[BDKK02] Becker, J.; Delfmann, P.; Knackstedt, R.; Kuropka, D.: Konfigurative Referenzmodellierung. In: Becker, J.; Knackstedt, R. (eds.): Wissensmanagement mit Referenzmodellen. Konzepte für die Anwendungssystem- und Organisationsgestaltung. Heidelberg 2002 pp. 25-144.

[BeSc04] Becker, J.; Schütte, R.: Handelsinformationssysteme. 2nd edition, Frankfurt am Main 2004.

[Böhm04] Böhmann, T.: Modularisierung von IT-Dienstleistungen – Eine Methode für das Service Engineering. Wiesbaden 2004.

[BöKr04a] Böhmann, T.; Krcmar, H.: Servicedatenmanagement für modulare Dienstleistungen. In: Luczak, H. (ed.): Betriebliche Tertiarisierung: Der ganzheitliche Wandel vom Produktionsbetrieb zum dienstleistenden Problemlöser. Wiesbaden 2004.

[BöKr04b] Böhmann, T.; Krcmar, H.: Grundlagen und Entwicklungstrends im IT-Servicemanagement. HMD – Praxis der Wirtschaftsinformatik (2004) 237, pp. 7-21.

[BöKr05] Böhmann, T.; Krcmar, H.: Einfach besser? Zur Anwendbarkeit des industriellen Komplexitätsmanagements auf variantenreiche IT-Dienstleistungen. In: Ferstl, O. K.; Sinz, E. J.; Eckert, S.; Isselhorst, T. (eds.): Wirtschaftsinformatik 2005: eEconomy, eGovernment, eSociety. Bamberg 2005, pp. 449-468.

[BöSK07] Böhmann, T.; Schermann, M.; Krcmar, H.: Reference Model Evaluation: Towards an Application-Oriented Approach. Forthcoming in: Fettke, P.; Loos, P. (eds.): Reference Modeling for Business Systems Analysis. Hershey et al. 2007.

[BrBu04] vom Brocke, J.; Buddendick, C.: Organisationsformen in der Referenzmodellierung: Forschungsbedarf und Gestaltungsempfehlungen auf Basis der Transaktionskostentheorie. Witschaftsinformatik 46 (2004) 5, pp. 341-352.

[BuMe01] Bullinger, H.-J.; Meiren, T.: Service Engineering. In: Bruhn, M.; Meffert, H. (eds.): Handbuch Dienstleistungsmanagement. Wiesbaden 2001, pp. 149-175.

[Burr00] Burr, W.: Modularisierung, Leistungstiefengestaltung und Systembündelung bei technischen Dienstleistungen: Ansätze zu einer ökonomischen Fundierung des Service Engineerings in Dienstleistungsunternehmen. Stuttgart 2000.

[BWFK04] Böhmann, T.; Winkler, T.; Fogl, F.; Krcmar, H.: Servicedatenmanagement für IT-Dienstleistungen: Ansatzpunkte für ein fachkonzeptionelles Referenzmodell. In: Becker, J.; Delfmann, P. (eds.): Referenzmodellierung: Grundlagen, Techniken und domänenbezogene Anwendung. Heidelberg 2004, pp. 99-124.

[DiHL96] Differding, C.; Hoisl, B.; Lott, C. M.: Technology Package for the Goal Question Metric Paradigm. Kaiserslautern 1996.

[FäAu03] Fähnrich, K.-P.; Auer, S.: Product Models in Service Engineering. In: Proceedings of the 17th International Conference on Production and Research 2003. Blacksburg 2003.

[Fähn98] Fähnrich, K.-P.: Service Engineering: Perspektiven einer noch jungen Fachdisziplin. Information Management & Consulting 13 (1998) 8, pp. 37-39.

[FeLo03a] Fettke, P.; Loos, P.: Multiperspective Evaluation of Reference Models – Towards a Framework. In: International Workshop on Conceptual Modeling Quality (IWCMQ'03). Chicago 2003.

[FeLo03b] Fettke, P; Loos, P.: Ontological evaluation of reference models using the Bunge-Wand-Weber-model. In: Proceedings of the 9$^{th}$ Americas Conference on Information Systems 2003. Tampa 2003.

[FeLo04a] Fettke, P.; Loos, P.: Referenzmodellierungsforschung. Wirtschaftsinformatik 46 (2004) 5, pp. 331-340.

[FeLo04b] Fettke, P.; Loos, P.: Systematische Erhebung von Referenzmodellen – Ergebnisse einer Voruntersuchung. In: Loos, P. (ed.): Working Papers of the Research Group Information Systems & Management. Mainz 2004.

[Fish97] Fisher, M. L.: What is the right supply chain for your product? Harvard Business Review 75 (1997) 2, p. 105.

[Fran98] Frank, U.: Die Evaluation von Artefakten: Eine zentrale Herausforderung der Wirtschaftsinformatik. In: Workshop Evaluation und Evaluationsforschung in der Wirtschaftsinformatik. Linz 1998.

[FWBK05] Fogl, F.; Winkler, T.; Böhmann, T.; Krcmar, H.: MoSES – Baukastensystem für modulare Dienstleistungen. In: Hermann, T.; Krcmar, H.; Kleinbeck, U. (eds.): Konzepte für das Service Engineering – Modularisierung, Prozessgestaltung und Produktivitätsmanagement. Heidelberg 2005, pp. 85-100.

[HeHä00] Heinrich, L. J.; Häntschel, I. (eds.): Evaluation und Evaluationsforschung in der Wirtschaftsinformatik. Munich 2000.

[Hein02] Heinrich, L. J.: Bedeutung von Evaluation und Evaluationsforschung in der Wirtschaftsinformatik. In: Heinrich, L. J.; Häntschel, I. (eds.): Evaluation und Evaluationsforschung in der Wirtschaftsinformatik. Munich 2002, pp. 7-22.

[HMPR04] Hevner, A. R.; March, S. T.; Park, J.; Ram, S.: Design Science in Information Systems Research. MIS Quarterly, 28 (2004) 1, pp. 75-105.

[HoKe97] Houdek, F.; Kempter, H.: Quality patterns – an approach to packaging software engineering experience. SIGSOFT Software Engineering Notes 22 (1997) 3, p. 81-88.

[Krom01] Kromrey, H.: Evaluation – ein vielschichtiges Konzept: Begriff und Methodik von Evaluierung und Evaluationsforschung, Empfehlungen für die Praxis. Sozialwissenschaften und Berufspraxis 24 (2001) 2, pp. 105-131.

[LoFe05] Loos, P.; Fettke, P.: Referenzmodellierung – Entwicklungsstand und Perspektiven. Information Management & Consulting 20 (2005) Sonderausgabe – 30 Jahre Wirtschaftsinformatik Saarbrücken – Arbeitsmarkt- und Innovationsmotor für Deutschland, pp. 21-26.

[Love04] Love, A.; Implementation Evaluation: In: Wholey, S.; Hatry, H. P.; Newcomer, K. E. (eds.): Handbook of practical program evaluation, J 2004. San Francisco 2004. pp. 63-97.

[MiZh00] Misic, V. B.; Zhao, J. L.: Evaluating the Quality of Reference Models. In: Leander, A. H. F.; Liddle, S. W.; Storey, V. C. (eds.): Conceptual Modeling – ER 2000: 19$^{th}$ International Conference on Conceptual Modeling. Lecture Notes in Computer Science. Berlin et al. 2000. pp. 484-498.

[Mohr82] Mohr, L. B.: Explaining Organizational Behavior: The Limits and Possibilities of Theory and Research. San Francisco 1982.

[OMG03] Object Management Group: OMG Unified Modeling Language Specification Version 1.5. 2003.

[Reek00] van Reeken, A. J.: Informationssysteme als Evaluationsobjekt: Einführung und Grundlegung. In: Heinrich, L. J.; Häntschel, I. (eds.): Evaluation und Evaluationsforschung in der Wirtschaftsinformatik. Munich 2002, pp. 49-58.

[RoSc97] Rosemann, M.; Schütte, R.: Grundsätze ordnungsmäßiger Referenzmodellierung. In: Becker, J.; Rosemann, M.; Schütte, R. (eds.): Entwicklungsstand und Entwicklungsperspektiven der Referenzmodellierung. Institut für Wirtschaftsinformatik der Westfälischen Wilhems-Universität Münster: Münster 1997, pp. 16-33.

[ScRo98] Schütte, R.; Rotthowe, T.: The Guidelines of Modeling – An Approach to Enhance the Quality in Information Models. In: Ling, T. W.; Ram, S.; Lee, M. L. (eds.): Proceedings of the 17th International Conference on Conceptual Modeling (ER 1998). Singapore 1998, p. 240-254.

[ScSW02] Scheer, A.-W.; Seel, C.; Wilhelm, G.: Entwicklungsstand in der Referenzmodellierung. Industrie Management 18 (2002) 1, pp. 9-12.

[Wang00] von Wangenheim, C.G., et al., Zielorientiertes Messen und Bewerten zur Software-Qualitätsverbesserung – Eine Kosten/Nutzen-Analyse. In: Heinrich, L. J.; Häntschel, I. (eds.): Evaluation und Evaluationsforschung in der Wirtschaftsinformatik. Munich 2002, pp. 253-266.

[Wild00] Wildemann, H. (ed.): Supply Chain Management. Munich 2000.

[WoJR90] Womack, J. P.; Jones, D. T.; Roos, D.: The Machine that Changed the World. New York 1990.

# Authors

## Prof. Dr. Wil M. P. van der Aalst

Eindhoven University of Technology
Department of Information Systems
PO Box 513, 5600 MB Eindhoven, The Netherlands
Phone: +31 40 2474295
Fax: +31 40 2432612
E-Mail: w.m.p.v.d.aalst@tue.nl

## Jun.-Prof. Dr. Frederik Ahlemann

European Business School
Department of Supply Chain Management & Information Systems
Rheingaustraße 1, 65375 Oestrich-Winkel, Germany
Phone: +49 6723 991274
Fax: +49 (0)6723 991259
E-Mail: frederik.ahlemann@ebs.de

## Prof. Dr. Jörg Becker

University of Münster
European Research Center for Information Systems
Leonardo-Campus 3, 48149 Münster, Germany
Phone: +49 251 83 38100
Fax: +49 251 83 38109
E-Mail: becker@ercis.uni-muenster.de

## Dr. Tilo Böhmann

Munich University of Technology
Department of Information Systems
Boltzmannstraße 3, 85748 Garching, Germany
Phone: +49 89 28919528
Fax: +49 89 28919533
E-Mail: boehmann@in.tum.de

## Dr. Patrick Delfmann

University of Münster
European Research Center for Information Systems
Leonardo-Campus 3, 48149 Münster, Germany
Phone: +49 251 83 38083
Fax: +49 251 83 28083
E-Mail: delfmann@ercis.uni-muenster.de

## Florian Gottschalk

Eindhoven University of Technology
Department of Information Systems
PO Box 513, 5600 MB Eindhoven, The Netherlands
Phone: +31 40 2475517
Fax: +31 40 2432612
E-Mail: f.gottschalk@tue.nl

## Dr. Monique H. Jansen-Vullers

Eindhoven University of Technology
Department of Information Systems
PO Box 513, 5600 MB Eindhoven, The Netherlands
Phone: +31 40 2474366
Fax: +31 40 2432612
E-Mail: m.h.jansen-vullers@tue.nl

## Dr. Ralf Knackstedt

University of Münster
European Research Center for Information Systems
Leonardo-Campus 3, 48149 Münster, Germany
Phone: +49 251 83 38094
Fax: +49 251 83 28094
E-Mail: knackstedt@ercis.uni-muenster.de

## Prof. Dr. Helmut Krcmar

Munich University of Technology
Department of Information Systems
Boltzmannstraße 3, 85748 Garching, Germany
Phone: +49 89 28919532
Fax: +49 89 28919533
E-Mail: krcmar@in.tum.de

## Tobias Rieke

University of Münster
European Research Center for Information Systems
Leonardo-Campus 3, 48149 Münster, Germany
Phone: +49 251 83 38072
Fax: +49 251 83 28072
E-Mail: rieke@ercis.uni-muenster.de

## Michael Schermann

Munich University of Technology
Department of Information Systems
Boltzmannstraße 3, 85748 Garching, Germany
Phone: +49 89 28919507
Fax: +49 89 28919533
E-Mail: michael.schermann@in.tum.de

## Christian Seel

Saarland University
Department of Information Systems
Stuhlsatzenhausweg 3, 66123 Saarbrücken, Germany
Tel.: +49 681 3025145
Fax: +49 681 3023696
E-Mail: ch.seel@iwi.uni-sb.de

## Dr. Oliver Thomas

Saarland University
Department of Information Systems
Stuhlsatzenhausweg 3, 66123 Saarbrücken, Germany
Tel.: +49 681 3025239
Fax: +49 681 3024786
E-Mail: thomas@iwi.uni-sb.de